W9-BFM-178

Your One-Stop
Guide to
Mary

Your One-Stop Guide to Mary

MITCH FINLEY

CHARIS

SERVANT PUBLICATIONS
ANN ARBOR, MICHIGAN

© 2000 by Mitch Finley
All rights reserved.

Charis Books is an imprint of Servant Publications especially designed to serve
Roman Catholics.

All quotations from Scripture are from the New Revised Standard Version Bible:
Catholic Edition, © 1993 and 1989, Division of Christian Education of the
National Council of Churches of Christ in the United States of America. Used
by permission. All rights reserved.

Excerpts from the English translation of the *Catechism of the Catholic Church* for
use in the United States of America. © 1994, United States Catholic
Conference, Inc.–Liberia Editrice Vaticana. Used with Permission.

The lyrics in the front of this book from John Stewart's song, "Star in the Black
Sky Shining," are © 1998 by John Stewart. Reprinted with permission. For a
catalog of John Stewart's recordings write: Homecoming Records, P.O. Box
2050, Malibu, CA 90265.

Servant Publications
P.O. Box 8617
Ann Arbor, MI 48107

Cover design: Hile Illustration and Design, Ann Arbor, Michigan

00 01 02 03 10 9 8 7 6 5 4 3 2 1

Printed in the United States of America
ISBN 1-56955-194-4

LIBRARY OF CONGRESS CATALOGING-IN-PUBLICATION DATA

Finley, Mitch.
    Your one-stop guide to Mary / by Mitch Finley.
        p. cm.
    Includes bibliographical references.
    ISBN 1-56955-194-4 (alk. paper)
    1. Mary, Blessed Virgin, Saint—Theology.   2. Catholic Church—Doctrines.
    I. Title.

BT602.F56 2000
232.91—dc21   00-035828

Dedication

In memory of my mother, who passed into eternal life on December 11, 1993, and whose middle name was Marie. She had a difficult life right down the line, but all things considered, it was a life she lived with remarkable unselfishness, grace, and equanimity. This one is for you, Mom.

Contents

There was a woman I saw on the street,

 I swear she was wearing the moon on her feet.

She said, "Do you know me?"

 I said, "I don't know."

She told me to listen and then I could go.

She said, "I am the course that the river is winding,

I am the horse that the angel is riding,

I am the source of the love you are finding.

Do you know who I am? It is blinding.

I am the star in the black sky shining."

═══════════════════════════════════════

John Stewart,
"Star in the Black Sky Shining"

Mary in Catholic Life

Is there any other woman in the history of Western civilization who has had as great an impact as Mary, the Mother of Jesus? Without a doubt, the answer is no. In the words of historian Jaroslav Pelikan:

> Even in the absence of reliable statistical data ... it is probably safe to estimate that for nearly two thousand years "Mary" has been the name most frequently given to girls at baptism, and, through the exclamation "Jesus, Mary, and Joseph" ... and above all through the *Ave Maria,* which has been repeated literally millions of times every day, the female name that has been pronounced most often in the Western world....

The Virgin Mary has been more of an inspiration to more people than any other woman who has ever lived. And she remains so as we enter the twenty-first century, despite its being conventionally regarded as secularistic by contrast with previous so-called ages of faith.[1]

Because of her close relationship with Jesus, from the Christian community's earliest days Mary attracted special attention from believers. Yet, as we shall see, the New Testament's understanding of Mary is far from homogenized.

That Mary was the Mother of the Messiah naturally attracted Christians to her. Yet it is the Christian doctrine of the communion of saints that has made it possible for Christians to relate to Mary as they have for two millennia. In a nutshell, this doctrine refers to the community of believers in time and in eternity. "The communion of saints is formed by the Holy Spirit into one body participating in Christ's life by Baptism."[2] Another name for the communion of saints is "the Mystical Body of Christ."[3] This doctrine means that all the faithful, in time and in eternity, belong to one community and continue to relate to one another. Just as we pray for one another on earth, so those who dwell in eternal light may pray for us, and we may ask them for their prayers. "Prayer asks the intercession of the saints with God, and honors God's holy creatures, so giving honor to the Creator, the source of all holiness."[4]

Mary is a fellow member of the communion of saints, but because of her privileged status as the Mother of Christ, chosen by God as the human mother of his Son, Mary holds pride of place among humans now in heaven. While she is a human being and in no way divine or even quasi-divine, down through history Mary has fired the Christian heart with an

Mary's Consent

Mary gave her consent in faith at the Annunciation and maintained it without hesitation at the foot of the Cross. Ever since, her motherhood has extended to the brothers and sisters of her Son "who still journey on earth surrounded by dangers and difficulties" [Vatican II, *Lumen Gentium*, n. 62]. Jesus, the only mediator, is the way of our prayer; Mary, his mother and ours, is wholly transparent to him: she "shows the way" ... and is herself "the Sign" of the way, according to the traditional iconography of East and West.

Catechism of the Catholic Church[5]

affection unmatched by any other saint.

Why do Catholicism, the Eastern Orthodox traditions, and to a lesser degree the Anglican churches honor Mary so highly? Christianity is a religion rather heavily laden with masculine images and metaphors.

God is neither male nor female. According to Genesis both male and female are created in God's image; therefore, we can learn something about God from both the masculine and the feminine. Christianity, however, is a religion that worships a loving Father-God, not a Mother-God. Reasons for this are deeply rooted in divine revelation and Christian tradition, reasons not as easily dismissed as those determined to impose a feminist theological ideology on Christianity would have us believe. Scripture scholar John W. Miller notes:

Not once in biblical tradition is God ever spoken of as "she" or "her" or regarded as genderless. On the other hand, God is not portrayed there simply as male either, but as a father whose tenderness and compassion are often mother-like. In no instance does this imply that God has become a mother-figure to his worshipers. The uniformity of the canonical representation of God as father is one of its most notable features.[6]

Mary is God's answer to Christianity's need for a strong feminine presence to balance its rootedness in a compassionate masculine Christ who unites us to a loving Father-God. Yet Mary is not a goddess but a fellow human being. She stands as the first model of faith and as an image of what all believers are called to be in this world. Through baptism we become adopted brothers and sisters of Christ. Therefore, his Father becomes our Father, and his mother becomes our Mother. Just as Jesus did during his earthly life, we turn to our divine Father and our human Mother who now dwells in eternal light and loves us with a mother's love for all her children. We turn to our loving Father-God as our Creator. We turn to our loving Mother, Mary, for her prayers on our behalf. This is the theological bottom line.

Catholicism has a warm spot in its heart for the Blessed Mother. She is there for us as a fully human mother; at the same time, she has a unique and special relationship with Christ and with our loving Father-God. She is there to speak up for us, as it were, and to care for us with her prayers. In no way does this belittle the compassion and love of Christ for us, nor does it suggest that we need something more in addition to Christ's saving action. Salvation is accomplished by Christ once and for all.

Christ gives us his mother as our Mother, too, as a special guide and companion. Yet there are no divisions. Mary's love for us is God's love for us, one and the same. When we honor the Mother, we honor the Son who came into the world through her "yes" and through her woman's body. When we honor Mary, we honor the God who created her. "As sailors are guided by a star to the port," said St. Thomas Aquinas in the thirteenth century, "so are Christians guided to heaven by Mary."[7]

If some Catholics' devotion to Mary has become unbalanced; if devotion to and veneration of Mary has slipped over into virtual worship of Mary—Mariolotry—this is clearly inappropriate. Official Catholic church teachings and responsible theologians scrupulously object. We *venerate* Mary, we do not worship her, because God alone is worthy of human worship.

New Testament Teaching About Mary

1. Mary is the human mother of Jesus (Matthew 1:18).
2. Mary is also the Mother of God (Elizabeth calls Mary "the mother of my Lord" Luke 1:43; Galatians 4:4-6).
3. Mary is the Mother of Jesus' disciples (John 19:26-27).
4. Mary is the Virgin Mother of Jesus (Matthew 1:18; Luke 1:34).
5. Mary is a disciple of Jesus (Acts 1:14; 2:1).
6. Jesus listens to his mother (John 2:3).

We honor Mary for her special role in the history of salvation, and we ask Mary for her prayers. We do not pray to Mary as if she had some power independent of the power of God.

The purpose of this book is to offer a basic introduction to Catholicism's devotion to and veneration of Mary, the Mother of Christ. It proposes to touch as many of the Marian "bases" as possible without turning into an in-depth scholarly study. While you may certainly read this book cover to cover, it will serve equally well as a resource to dip into when you have specific questions about Mary or about Catholicism's Marian practices, beliefs, and traditions.

The author will be well pleased if you gain from this small book a healthy, warm, trusting affection for Mary, the Mother of Jesus, who is our Mother, too.

CHAPTER ONE

Mary in the Scriptures

The most important information we have about Mary comes from the New Testament, the early church's divinely inspired witness to the unrepeatable foundational events of the Christian faith. On the one hand, it is significant that Mary plays such a major role in salvation history. On the other hand, Mary appears in only a few New Testament texts, so we learn relatively little about her, and much of it exists for theological rather than historical purposes. What we do learn, however, has been enough to keep devotion to Mary alive and thriving for some two thousand years.

In this chapter we will single out the New Testament texts that refer to Mary in some way, looking at them more or less in the order in which they were written. We will see what each contributes to our understanding of Mary and her role in Christian life and faith.

Galatians 4:4-6
But when the fullness of time had come, God sent his Son, born of a woman, born under the law, in order to redeem those who were under the law, so that we might receive adoption as children. And because you are children, God has sent the Spirit of his Son into our hearts, crying, "Abba! Father!"

Scripture scholars date the Letter of St. Paul to the Galatians to about the year A.D. 54, which places it among the earliest New Testament documents.[1] This means that the first mention of Mary in the New Testament does not occur, as one might expect, in one of the four Gospels telling the story of Jesus' life and ministry. It is particularly significant that Paul does not mention Mary by name but, rather, refers to her role in the history of salvation and her identity as the human mother of the Son of God.

Paul makes the theological point that the Son of God was "born of a woman." This is who Mary is, the Mother of the Son of God. Everything else we know about her, and everything else we believe about her, stems from this most basic theological observation. So important is this fact that Paul feels no need to mention Mary by name. Does this mean that Paul was nothing but a calculating intellectual with no sensitivity to the personal dimension? On the contrary. Notice, neither does Paul mention Jesus by name. He has no interest in naming names; he knows that his readers are perfectly aware of who he is talking about.

Paul continues by explaining that it is through this "woman" that we become the adopted sons and daughters of God, the brothers and sisters of Christ. Because Mary is the Mother of Jesus, we can become who we become through baptism, "children" of God with Christ as our brother. In other words, no Mary, no Jesus; no Jesus, no accomplishment of "salvation," that is, spiritual liberation and healing for this life and the next. Who could deny that we owe an eternal debt of gratitude to Mary, the Mother of Jesus?

Paul declares that Jesus was "born of a woman," highlighting the *humanity* of the Son of God. The Christ did not appear in time and space, out of nowhere on the run, with a little "pop!" full-grown and ready for action. On the contrary, Paul insists. Jesus joined the human race in the way all human

The Six "Words" of Mary

Mary speaks only six times in the entire New Testament:
1. "How can this be, since I am a virgin?" (Luke 1:34).
2. "Here am I, the servant of the Lord: let it be with me according to your word" (Luke 1:38).
3. "My soul magnifies the Lord ... " (The Magnificat; Luke 1:47-55).
4. "Child, why have you treated us like this? Look, your father and I have been searching for you in great anxiety" (Luke 2:48).
5. "They have no wine" (John 2:3).
6. "Do whatever he tells you" (John 2:5).

beings do. He was born into the world from a human mother, a young woman—very young by today's standards, between fourteen and sixteen years old—and he sucked sweet human milk from her breasts.

Does this scandalize us? If so, it shouldn't. It did not scandalize St. Paul, and it obviously did not scandalize God, who evidently thought it was a great idea. As with later official Catholic declarations about Mary, this earliest mention of her by Paul makes a point about Christ: that the Son of God was as human as he could be.

At the same time, Paul makes a clear—and to his first readers, perhaps, a startling—connection. He says that Jesus is *God's* Son "born of a woman." Right there, in a nutshell, we have the doctrine that will be pronounced in a more technical theological fashion by the Council of Chalcedon in the fifth century, that Jesus was and is fully human *and* fully divine.

Because Jesus is God's Son, he is divine. Because he is Mary's son, he is also human. In this we can rejoice.

Mark 3:31-35

Then his mother and his brothers came; and standing outside, they sent to him and called him. A crowd was sitting around him; and they said to him, "Your mother and your brothers and sisters are outside, asking for you." And he replied, "Who are my mother and my brothers?" And looking at those who sat around him, he said, "Here are my mother and my brothers! Whoever does the will of God is my brother and sister and mother." (See parallels in Matthew 12:46 and Luke 8:19.)

Chronologically, the second mention of Mary in the New Testament occurs early in the Gospel of Mark. Scholarly consensus identifies Mark as the oldest of the four Gospels, probably written in the late sixties. This date would mean that some ten years after Paul first mentioned Mary in his Letter to the Galatians, the author of Mark still thinks she is important enough to include in his account of Jesus' life.

As typically interpreted, Mark's little drama doesn't seem to place the mother of Jesus in a positive light. The Mary who appears here doesn't seem to get a rave review even from her own son. Jesus seems to say that being his mother is no big deal. He doesn't exactly fall all over himself to be deferential to her or show her respect in public.

But take a closer look. A few verses earlier, Jesus' "family" had tried to "restrain" him, for people were saying that he was "out of his mind" (3:21). Mary and other relatives of Jesus may have been concerned that he might be harmed by the crowds.

So Jesus' remark in verses 33-35 ("Who are my mother and my brothers?" etc.) may have been his way to deflect a well-meant disruption and turn it into a "teachable moment." If you read this narrative closely, you see that at no point does Jesus show any direct or implied disrespect for his mother.

By including this story, Mark's Gospel teaches that even in her role as the human mother of Christ, what matters most about Mary is her faith and her obedience to the will of God. In this sense, Mark's Jesus does praise and honor his mother indirectly, for she is the prototypical disciple who became his mother precisely by giving herself over completely to the will of God.

Mark 6:3
Is not this the carpenter, the son of Mary ... ?
(See parallel in Matthew 13:55.)

This is the only other mention of Mary in Mark's Gospel, and only here does Mark refer to Mary by name. Those who are "astounded" (6:2) by Jesus' words may, in fact, be insulting him by identifying him with his mother. Jews were typically known by their fathers' names ("son of Joseph"), not their mothers' names. At the same time, Mark may intend a double meaning, both a historical reference and a theological affirmation of Mary's motherhood of Jesus.

Matthew 1:18-25
Now the birth of Jesus the Messiah took place in this way. When his mother Mary had been engaged to Joseph, but before they lived together, she was found to be with child from the Holy Spirit. Her husband Joseph, being a righteous

man and unwilling to expose her to public disgrace, planned to dismiss her quietly. But just when he had resolved to do this, an angel of the Lord appeared to him in a dream and said, "Joseph, son of David, do not be afraid to take Mary as your wife, for the child conceived in her is from the Holy Spirit. She will bear a son, and you are to name him Jesus, for he will save his people from their sins." All this took place to fulfill what had been spoken by the Lord through the prophet:

"Look, the virgin shall conceive and bear a son, and they shall name him Emmanuel," which means, "God is with us."

When Joseph awoke from sleep, he did as the angel of the Lord commanded him; he took her as his wife, but had no marital relations with her until she had borne a son; and he named him Jesus.

The Gospel of Matthew names Mary as the Mother of Jesus in its genealogy (1:16), but this later account is her big debut. Scholars date Matthew between 85 and 90 which puts it some twenty-five years after Mark and thirty-five years after Galatians. The Christian community has had time to reflect on Mary, her relationship to Jesus, and her meaning to the ongoing faith of the church. Mary has had time to become significant to Christians not only for her "function" as the mother of Jesus, but for herself as well. In Matthew she is shown as a witness to faith and discipleship.

The primary purpose of these lines from Matthew 1 is to establish the supernatural character of Jesus' conception and birth. Matthew doesn't go into any detail, as will Luke. He simply states what happened. In fact, Joseph is the "star" of Matthew's account of Jesus' birth, not Mary. Joseph the dreamer, Joseph the risk-taker. It is he who receives the message from the angel.

Matthew's Mary does not speak. Matthew talks *about* Mary, but Joseph is the one who receives angelic messages, and Joseph is the one who acts on faith. In the Gospel of Matthew, we may take Joseph as a model for the people of God, as in faith the church honors and cherishes Mary, the Mother of Jesus, down through the centuries to the present time.

At the same time, it is clear that Matthew sees the virginal conception of Jesus as the fulfillment of the prophet's words from Isaiah 7:14.

Matthew 2:10-11
When [the wise men] saw that the star had stopped, they were overwhelmed with joy. On entering the house, they saw the child with Mary his mother; and they knelt down and paid him homage. Then, opening their treasure chests, they offered him gifts of gold, frankincense, and myrrh.

One theme of Matthew's Gospel is its interest in showing that the gift of salvation is universal. The gentile wise men, or Magi, represent this all-inclusive perspective in Matthew. The Magi arrive soon after the birth of Jesus, and they bring him gifts, which later tradition interpreted as signifying Christ's kingship, divinity, and redemptive suffering (or virtue, prayer, and suffering).[2]

The Magi model a theologically solid devotion to Mary as they worship Christ in the presence of his mother. They worship the Christ child in the presence of Mary, which is a good way to describe how devotion to Mary should happen. Whenever we pray to Mary, it is always in the context of the worship that may be offered to Christ alone. We do not turn to Mary as if she has some power independent of the saving power of Christ. Rather, we turn to her only in the context of her—and our—relationship with Christ in faith. Mary can never be separated from Jesus, her son.

Mary's presence continues in verses 13-15 and 19-21, but Matthew simply tells us, again, that she and "the child" are in Joseph's care.

Luke 1:26-29

In the sixth month the angel Gabriel was sent by God to a town in Galilee called Nazareth, to a virgin engaged to a man whose name was Joseph, of the house of David. The virgin's name was Mary. And he came to her and said, "Greetings, favored one! The Lord is with you." But she was much perplexed by his words and pondered what sort of greeting this might be.

The Gospel of Luke offers the most fully developed teaching on Mary in the entire New Testament, yet always in conjunction with its attention to its teaching on Christ. Scholars date Luke's Gospel—and its companion document the Acts of the Apostles—to about the same period as Matthew.[3]

This means that the early church has had some fifty years to reflect upon the meaning and place of Mary in the life and spirituality of the Christian community. The author of Luke-Acts was able to draw upon this emerging Marian tradition while contributing his own insights. This he did in the most theologically rich portrait of Mary we have.

In Luke's Gospel, Mary, not Joseph, takes center stage. In one of the most dramatic and remarkable scenes in all of

Scripture, the angel Gabriel, sent by God, greets a virgin named Mary in a most dignified manner, addressing her as "favored one." Luke establishes Mary's status not only at the time of the visit from the angel, but for his own time and, by extension, for all times. Mary is singled out by God to play a special part in salvation history; once this fact is established, it cannot change.

For Luke's Gospel, Mary is the "favored one" not just temporarily until she has served an immediate purpose, but yesterday, today, and forever. Otherwise there would be no reason, some fifty years after the death and resurrection of Christ, to portray Mary in such an exalted manner. Mary's meaning and purpose continues because of her unique role as the Mother of the Savior.

Luke also makes it clear that Jesus' conception has a supernatural character. For Mary, he says twice, is a "virgin." Luke says nothing about a theoretical superiority of virginity or celibacy over marriage. That is not the topic at all. Luke's intention is, rather, to make a point about the extraordinary character of Jesus' conception and birth. Though he does not mention Mary by name, Luke makes the point again in Luke 3:23, where he says that Jesus is "thought" to be the son of Joseph.

Jesus is born of a human mother, yes; but she is a virgin. In other words, even though Mary's virginity is factual, Luke's point is theological, not physiological. Luke would, no doubt, have been taken aback by later use of Mary's virginity to promote negative attitudes toward marriage and sex.

This first part of Luke's account of the encounter between the angel Gabriel and Mary concludes with Luke's comment that Mary "was much perplexed by his words and pondered what sort of greeting this might be." Talk about an understatement. "Much perplexed," indeed! We might say she was "blown away." Anyway, that leads directly into the next phase of the encounter.

Luke 1:30-34

The angel said to her, "Do not be afraid, Mary, for you have found favor with God. And now, you will conceive in your womb and bear a son, and you will name him Jesus. He will be great, and will be called the Son of the Most High, and the Lord God will give to him the throne of his ancestor David. He will reign over the house of Jacob forever, and of his kingdom there will be no end." Mary said to the angel, "How can this be, since I am a virgin?"

Without Mary saying a word, Gabriel knows that his appearance and greeting have blown young Mary's mind; and now she is clueless. First the angel offers reassurance. Then he blows her mind again, telling her that she will become pregnant, that her child will be "Son of the Most High," and so forth. Now Mary is more than "much perplexed," and she is not shy about saying so. She has a question, and she wants an answer. She knows the score, and she knows she has not been doing what a girl must do to get pregnant. So what gives?

No shy, retiring, passive, acquiescent wallflower, Mary. Angel or no angel, she has her question, and she wants an answer. Young Mary has no need for assertiveness training. From this we may take the lesson that faith and questions go hand in hand. You can have faith and still have your questions, even your doubts. Just like young Mary.

Luke 1:35-38

The angel said to her, "The Holy Spirit will come upon you, and the power of the Most High will overshadow you; therefore the child to be born will be holy; he will be called Son of God. And now, your relative Elizabeth in her old age has also conceived a son; and this is the sixth month for her who was said to be barren. For nothing will be impossible with God." Then Mary said, "Here am I, the servant of the Lord; let it be with me according to your word." Then the angel departed from her.

The angel Gabriel shows neither surprise nor irritation at Mary's question. He briefly explains what will happen. Note that Gabriel's explanation of how Mary is going to conceive is no precise scientific explanation. Rather, his words fill the air, and young Mary's heart, with mystery. Then we get a few details about her aged relative Elizabeth. The bottom line: Nothing is impossible with God.

With not much to go on, only the mysterious words of a mysterious angel, Mary signs on, opens herself and her life to God's "whatever" based on trust alone. She is God's servant, so let it all happen to her according to God's plan as outlined by the angel. She still doesn't understand, but now she does have a clue, which is about as much as anyone can expect.

Luke 1:39-45

In those days Mary set out and went with haste to a Judean town in the hill country, where she entered the house of Zechariah and greeted Elizabeth. When Elizabeth heard Mary's greeting, the child leaped in her womb. And Elizabeth was filled with the Holy Spirit and exclaimed with a loud cry, "Blessed are you among women, and blessed is the fruit of your womb. And why has this happened to me, that the mother of my Lord comes to me? For as soon as I heard the sound of your greeting, the child in my womb leaped for joy. And blessed is she who believed that there would be a fulfillment of what was spoken to her by the Lord."

Luke's Gospel does not say that young Mary immediately dropped everything and hurried off to visit her relative Elizabeth. It just says "in those days." But, assuming the historical nature of this anecdotal material—a big assumption, indeed—we may presume that not many days after her encounter with the angel Gabriel Mary left Nazareth for Elizabeth's place. We don't know exactly where Elizabeth and Zechariah lived, but evidently it was within walking distance for young Mary.

The Mary who visits Elizabeth is greeted and immediately surprised. Here she has made the trek to see Elizabeth, having just heard by angel of Elizabeth's pregnancy. What does the older woman do but turn Mary's arrival into an opportunity to sing her younger relative's praises? "Filled with the Holy Spirit," the infant John the Baptizer does somersaults in Elizabeth's womb; Elizabeth somehow knows that young Mary is expecting her own bundle of joy, and this is far from your average pregnancy.

Immediately Elizabeth praises Mary and the child she carries, and she protests her own unworthiness to be visited by the mother of "my Lord." Elizabeth knows what's going on, because her own child "leaped for joy" in her womb. Finally, she praises young Mary for her faith, which is the heart of the matter, Mary-wise. Elizabeth sets an example for all Christians, down to our own time, when she praises Mary for her faith. For this is one of Mary's main reasons for being: to act as a model of faith for all believers, all disciples of her son, the Lord Jesus. Elizabeth might as well have said, "Pay attention to young Mary's faith, and go and do likewise."

Luke 1:46-55

And Mary said, "My soul magnifies the Lord, and my spirit rejoices in God my Savior, for he has looked with favor on the lowliness of his servant. Surely, from now on all generations will call me blessed; for the Mighty One has done great things for me, and holy is his name. His mercy is for those who fear him from generation to generation. He has shown strength with his arm; he has scattered the proud in the thoughts of their hearts. He has brought down the powerful from their thrones, and lifted up the lowly; he has filled the hungry with good things, and sent the rich away empty. He has helped his servant Israel, in remembrance of his mercy, according to the promise he made to our ancestors, to Abraham and to his descendants forever."

Young Mary deflects Elizabeth's praise from herself to God. Traditionally called the Magnificat—from the first word in the Latin translation—Mary's hymn of praise is one of the most beautiful and most familiar parts of the New Testament. Those who pray the Liturgy of the Hours pray the Magnificat every day as a part of Vespers (Evening Prayer). Once again, the Gospel of Luke presents Mary as a model for all believers.

At the same time, Luke presents the early church's understanding of Mary and her unique place in salvation history. From the time of Luke-Acts onward, the church's understanding of Mary places her in a privileged position. When read slowly, line by line, the Magnificat encapsulates this understanding beautifully. Indeed, the key to all later Christian understandings of Mary occurs in a couple of lines from the Magnificat: "from now on all generations will call me blessed; for the Mighty One has done great things for me, and holy is his name."

We honor Mary because she is uniquely blessed; she was chosen by God to be the human mother of his Son. The "Mighty One" did "great things" for Mary, therefore she deserves for "all generations" to call her "blessed." This is what the Gospel of Luke teaches about Mary. To repeat, this is the richest, most fully developed teaching on Mary in the entire New Testament.

At the same time, Mary is true to form, for in most of the Magnificat she continues to deflect attention from herself to God. She sings of God's "mercy" and "strength"; indeed, the Magnificat begins and ends with praise for God's mercy. At the same time, the Magnificat is clearly countercultural, because it reverses the values of the world by declaring that God blesses the poor and lowly while sending the rich away with nothing. It was Mary's "lowliness" that God found attractive.

Luke 2:1-7

In those days a decree went out from Emperor Augustus that all the world should be registered. This was the first registration and was taken while Quirinius was governor of Syria. All went to their own towns to be registered. Joseph also went from the town of Nazareth in Galilee to Judea, to the city of David called Bethlehem, because he was descended from the house and family of David. He went to be registered with Mary, to whom he was engaged and who was expecting a child. While they were there, the time came for her to deliver her child. And she gave birth to her firstborn son and wrapped him in bands of cloth, and laid him in a manger, because there was no place for them in the inn.

The simplicity of the birth narrative in Luke's Gospel is utterly disarming. If we look for profound theological insights, we may be put off by what a plain and simple story it is. Luke explains why Joseph and Mary were in Bethlehem, then in the last two sentences he states what happened. If anything, Luke merely illustrates what Paul says in the Letter to the Galatians, that the Son of God was "born of a woman." Instead of *telling* us, as Paul does, the Gospel of Luke *shows* us that the Son of God was "born of a woman." Once again, Mary's role is to show us the full and complete humanity of God's Son.

Centuries of romanticizing the situation aside, Luke's Gospel shows us in simple, almost stark terms that Jesus was born in the plainest of settings. The Son of God came into the world not amidst power and wealth but in poverty and lowliness. His mother was a girl of no worldly account, and Joseph, who would act as his father in every sense of the word except the biological one, was equally obscure. Only from Matthew 13:55 ("Is not this [i.e., Jesus] the carpenter's son?") do we get the information that Joseph was a carpenter. Mary and Joseph were, for all practical purposes, homeless at the time of Jesus' birth. There is no indication, however, that Mary coped with this situation with anything but equanimity and trust in God. We see no indication that Mary complained about the less-than-ideal birthing situation.

Sometimes people interpret "firstborn son" to mean that Mary had other sons after Jesus was born. But "firstborn" is simply a legal description to indicate that in the society of his time Jesus had the rights and privileges of a firstborn son.[4]

Luke 2:16-19

So [the shepherds] went with haste and found Mary and Joseph, and the child lying in the manger. When they saw this, they made known what had been told them about this child; and all who heard it were amazed at what the shepherds told them. But Mary treasured all these words and pondered them in her heart.

The Mary of the encounter with the shepherds does not speak. She listens. In one of the most familiar lines from all of Scripture, Luke tells us that she "treasured all these words and pondered them in her heart." Mary hears the shepherds' account of what they learned out in the fields from angels, that "to you is born this day ... a Savior, who is the Messiah, the Lord" (2:11). Added to what she heard from the angel Gabriel about her child's conception and who he would be, this gives Mary more than enough to treasure, more than enough to ponder.

A traditional interpretation of Luke's remark about Mary treasuring and pondering casts her in the role of the prototypical Christian contemplative. Mary prayerfully meditates upon the mysteries of Jesus' conception, birth, and identity. While the actual text may or may not warrant this interpretation, countless generations have been inspired to prayerful contemplation by Luke's remark about Mary.

Luke 2:22-35

When the time came for their purification according to the law of Moses, they brought him up to Jerusalem to present him to the Lord (as it is written in the law of the Lord, "Every firstborn male shall be designated as holy to the Lord"), and they offered a sacrifice according to what is stated in the law of the Lord, "a pair of turtledoves or two young pigeons."

Now there was a man in Jerusalem whose name was Simeon; this man was righteous and devout, looking forward to the consolation of Israel, and the Holy Spirit rested on him. It had been revealed to him by the Holy Spirit that he would not see death before he had seen the Lord's Messiah.

Guided by the Spirit, Simeon came into the temple; and when the parents brought in the child Jesus, to do for him what was customary under the law, Simeon took him in his arms and praised God, saying, "Master, now you are dismissing your servant in peace, according to your word; for my eyes have seen your salvation, which you have prepared in the presence of all peoples, a light for revelation to the Gentiles and for glory to your people Israel."

And the child's father and mother were amazed at what was being said about him. Then Simeon blessed them and said to his mother Mary, "This child is destined for the falling and the rising of many in Israel, and to be a sign that will be opposed so that the inner thoughts of many will be revealed—and a sword will pierce your own soul too."

The climax of Luke's narrative here is Simeon's announcement to young Mary. Written some fifty years after the death and resurrection of Jesus, Simeon's words draw on later events, projecting them back in time so Simeon appears to foretell the future. Mary's child will be a source of division.

Popular piety often interprets Simeon's final words, spoken directly to Mary—"and a sword will pierce your own soul too"—as a reference to the suffering she will undergo as a witness to her son's death. More likely, Luke's purpose is to point out that "Mary, too, the model believer, will have to decide for or against God's revelation in Jesus; [for] family ties do not create faith."[5]

While we may be reluctant to give up this interpretation—indeed, there is some validity to it—we may gain more if we reflect on the idea that Mary herself had to choose to believe in Jesus. We may think that there was no question for Mary about her son's identity. Did not the angel Gabriel tell her, flat-out, who her child would be? Did not the shepherds reaffirm this with their account of a message from angels about her son? We need to keep in mind, however, that the narratives of Jesus'

Jesus' Brothers?

The New Testament sometimes speaks of the "brothers" of Jesus. Does this mean Mary gave birth to other children, indicating she was not a lifelong virgin?

The Church has always understood these passages as not referring to other children of the Virgin Mary. In fact James and Joseph, "brothers of Jesus," are the sons of another Mary, a disciple of Christ, whom St. Matthew significantly calls "the other Mary" [Matthew 13:55; 27:56]. They are close relations of Jesus, according to an Old Testament expression.

Catechism of the Catholic Church[6]

infancy, in both Luke and Matthew, are more theological than historical. They are true in the sense that they teach the truth about Jesus, but they are less reliable if we seek historically accurate information.

Even if the purpose of the story about the meeting in the temple is more to pass along religious truth than historical facts, Simeon's final words to Mary reflect Luke's awareness that the historical Mary, like all believers, needed to choose to believe or not believe, to have faith or not have faith. Simeon's words suggest that for Mary this was not an easy choice but a difficult and painful one. We may gather encouragement and inspiration from this. We struggle with faith just as Mary, the model believer, struggled with faith.

Luke 2:39-51

When they had finished everything required by the law of the Lord, they returned to Galilee, to their own town of Nazareth. The child grew and became strong, filled with wisdom; and the favor of God was upon him.

Now every year his parents went to Jerusalem for the festival of the Passover. And when he was twelve years old, they went up as usual for the festival. When the festival was ended and they started to return, the boy Jesus stayed behind in Jerusalem, but his parents did not know it. Assuming that he was in the group of travelers, they went a day's journey. Then they started to look for him among their relatives and friends. When they did not find him, they returned to Jerusalem to search for him.

After three days they found him in the temple, sitting among the teachers, listening to them and asking them questions. And all who heard him were amazed at his understanding and his answers. When his parents saw him they were astonished; and his mother said to him, "Child, why have you treated us like this? Look, your father and I have been searching for you in great anxiety."

He said to them, "Why were you searching for me? Did you not know that I must be in my Father's house?" But they did not understand what he said to them. Then he went down with them and came to Nazareth, and was obedient to them. His mother treasured all these things in her heart.

Both Mary and Joseph are present in this narrative about Jesus lost and found. But Joseph remains silent. Only Mary and the boy Jesus speak, and the Gospel of Luke clearly focuses on Mary. It's easy to keep our eyes from seeing how ordinary and typical the family interactions are in this story. Pay close attention.

Mary and Joseph are a day's journey down the road before they realize that Jesus is missing. That means it takes them another day's journey to return to Jerusalem. Then they search for the boy for three days. This means that Jesus has been lost for *five days* before Mary and Joseph find him. Notice, too, that the temple is the last, not the first, place they look for him. They do not instinctively think of the temple as a place where Jesus would go to hang out. In other words, Mary and Joseph were not raising a twelve-year-old Jewish holier-than-thou kid. There must have been dozens of other places Mary and Joseph looked first.

Notice, too, how understated the whole story is. When Mary and Joseph finally do find the boy Jesus, Mary says, "Look, your father and I have been searching for you in great anxiety." After five days, Mary and Joseph must have been frantic. But all Luke has Mary say is "great anxiety." To say the least!

In the final lines of the story, Luke tells us that Mary and Joseph did not understand Jesus, yet Jesus was obedient to them. For the second time Luke tells us that Mary "treasured" all that had happened, a tip-off, perhaps, about the attitude Luke wants to encourage in those who read his Gospel. Thus, Mary would serve, again, as a model of faith.

John 2:1-5

On the third day there was a wedding in Cana of Galilee, and the mother of Jesus was there. Jesus and his disciples had also been invited to the wedding. When the wine gave out, the mother of Jesus said to him, "They have no wine." And Jesus said to her, "Woman, what concern is that to you and to me? My hour has not yet come." His mother said to the servants, "Do whatever he tells you."

Scholarly consensus dates the Gospel of John to the late nineties. John was the last of the four Gospels written down. We may presume, then, that when Mary appears in the fourth Gospel—two times only—we benefit from long reflection on her meaning to the church and to the spiritual life of Christians. As we shall see, however, the Mary of John's Gospel is a shadowy figure. The Gospel of John never uses her name, referring to her as "his mother," and "the mother of Jesus."

All the same, "the mother of Jesus" is an essential part of John's account of the wedding at Cana. At the very least, it places Jesus and his mother in a unique juxtaposition. We read, first, that "the mother of Jesus was there." Then, if not as an afterthought at least in a secondary sense, the writer adds that "Jesus and his disciples had also been invited."

Mary, not Jesus, notices that all the wine is gone. Although her words to Jesus are ambiguous, Mary evidently believes that Jesus can do something about the situation, otherwise she would not speak to him about it. Still, she does not tell Jesus *what to do* about the lack of wine. She does not say, "Son, they're out of wine. Run down to the wine merchant and get some more." She merely describes the situation. "They have no wine." She leaves it up to Jesus to do whatever he thinks is best.

Jesus' response to his mother is ambiguous, too. Translated literally, his words are "what to me and to you, woman." This phrase may "carry overtones of refusal or at least unwillingness to get involved in whatever the petitioner is concerned about."[7] Scholars think that the writer may have placed the next sentence on Jesus' lips, "My hour has not yet come," perhaps in an attempt to resolve some of the ambiguity in the previous remark.[8] Either way, Jesus does not reply to his mother's remark by asking what she wants him to do.

Jesus' mother is unfazed. Without responding directly to Jesus, and without presuming to tell him what to do, she speaks to the servants. "Do whatever he tells you." This leaves the door wide open for Jesus to do whatever he wants to do. At the same time, it's clear that Jesus' mother puts her trust in him to deal with the situation as he sees best.

Conceivably Jesus could have said almost anything. He could have said, "Go to the wine merchant and buy some more wine." Or, "What do you think—that I can produce wine out of thin air?" Instead, his response shows both a son's respect for his mother and a friend's compassion for the newlyweds, to spare them the embarrassment of running out of wine.

Jesus chooses to turn water into wine. But the scene is "set up" by Jesus' mother, who (a) notices that the wine supply is depleted; (b) speaks to Jesus about it; (c) ignores Jesus' initial rebuff; and (d) trusts him implicitly to do what is best.

More than likely, the fourth Gospel intends Mary's instructions, "Do whatever he tells you," for all who read or hear these words. Mary is a key figure in this story. Clearly the human author(s) of the fourth Gospel say something important here about Mary and about her place in the lives of all Christians. We can turn to her in our needs, asking for her prayers on our behalf. Just as she trusted Jesus to do what was best, so we need to trust that she will do what's best, too. For her will is one with the will of her son who is the risen Christ.

John 19:25b-27

Meanwhile, standing near the cross of Jesus were his mother, and his mother's sister, Mary the wife of Clopas, and Mary Magdalene. When Jesus saw his mother and the disciple whom he loved standing beside her, he said to his mother, "Woman, here is your son." Then he said to the disciple, "Here is your mother." And from that hour the disciple took her into his own home.

Only the Gospel of John relates this crucifixion encounter. The traditional Catholic interpretation of this passage is that the beloved disciple is a stand-in, as it were, for all of us. Dying on the cross, Jesus gives his mother to us as our Mother, and he gives all of us to his mother as her children and his brothers and sisters. Like the beloved disciple, we are to welcome the Mother of Jesus into our lives.

It's possible to take all this too literally, or in too maudlin a manner. Scripture scholars are uncertain how much symbolism the fourth Gospel means to attach to Jesus' words giving his mother and the beloved disciple to each other.[9]

A traditional Catholic interpretation of this scene suggests that for the Gospel of John there is a significant relationship between the Mother of Jesus and those who follow Christ and share in his risen life. No matter what else we do with regard to the Mother of Jesus, we may not ignore her completely—any more than he would ignore her completely—and claim to follow her son, living as a member of his body, the church.

Acts 1:13-14

When they had entered the city, they went to the room upstairs where they were staying, Peter, and John, and James, and Andrew, Philip and Thomas, Bartholomew and Matthew, James son of Alphaeus, and Simon the Zealot, and Judas son of James. All these were constantly devoting themselves to prayer, together with certain women, including Mary the mother of Jesus, as well as his brothers.

Mary is mentioned one more time in the New Testament, in the Acts of the Apostles, the companion document to the Gospel of Luke and contemporary with it, meaning it was written about 85 to 90. Acts identifies Mary as "the mother of Jesus," leaving no doubt about her presence with the eleven disciples after Jesus' ascension and prior to Pentecost. Together with "certain women," Mary is with the earliest group of believers, joining them in prayer "constantly."

Mary, the Mother of Jesus, is with the disciples as they wait in prayer for the coming of the Holy Spirit at Pentecost. They wait in sheer faith, and Mary waits with them. Notice, Mary does not claim to have any special insights into anything. She is simply there, in faith and in companionship. Soon Peter will

Mary's Enduring Virginity

The enduring virginity of Mary is something that goes beyond any documentary attestation that we have and represents praise of Mary that stems from our faith. We Roman Catholics consider it a doctrine of the church, but that does not necessarily mean that Mary told anyone that she always remained a virgin. We accept the doctrine of the "Ever Virgin" not on the basis of a biblical text, but from Christian reflection on the sanctity of Mary and the way in which that sanctity was expressed in her life.

Raymond E. Brown, S.S.[10]

stand up and deliver his famous sermon, explaining and interpreting the death and resurrection of Jesus. Soon Matthias will be chosen to replace the defector, Judas. No further mention will be made of Mary, the Mother of Jesus. Neither does she try to claim a leadership role based on being the Mother of the Messiah. She is simply there, in prayer and in community.

We might take this final appearance of Mary as a reminder. Mary does not try to move in and take over for her departed son. She is content to be a member of the little community of men and women who wait and pray. This might remind us that neither should we try to make of her more than she is. She is not an "assistant Messiah." She is no kind of goddess. She is one of the community of believers, she is one with us in faith. "Between the cross and the upper room," wrote Sally Cunneen, "Mary mastered her grief in order to transfer her dedication to the wider community of her son's followers. She is a true figure of human wisdom."[11]

As the Mother of the Savior, Mary holds a privileged position. In a church with a male Redeemer, she brings an important female presence, whose faith and trust in God opened the door for the coming of the Son of God into human history. She is a vitally important maternal presence for all believers, our Mother and companion in prayer. She is, indeed, the Blessed Mother. Her son is both fully divine and fully human, and we turn to him as both Savior and Brother. Mary, the Mother of Jesus, joins us in faith as we turn to her son in all our needs. She never wants to replace him in our affections, only to join us in our faith in God's unconditional, unlimited love.

The Book of Revelation

After the pre-Pentecost mention of Mary in Acts 1:13-14, she disappears from the Scriptures. You may ask, but what about Revelation 12:1? Isn't Mary the unnamed "woman clothed with the sun"?

A great portent appeared in heaven: a woman clothed with the sun, with the moon under her feet, and on her head a crown of twelve stars.

To this day, writers, artists, and illustrators often present Mary with a crescent moon at her feet and twelve stars forming a halo or crown over her head. Being apocalyptic, the Book of Revelation easily lends itself to misinterpretation. To see the Mother of Jesus in the "woman clothed with the sun" is innocent religious romanticism. Yet contemporary New Testament scholars are virtually unanimous in agreeing that the "woman clothed with the sun" is not a reference to Mary but an image of "the heavenly Israel, the spouse of God."[12]

Mary in the Hebrew Scriptures

From the time of the early fathers of the church, certain texts from the Hebrew Scriptures, or Old Testament, were interpreted as prophetic foreshadowings of the Mother of the Messiah.[13] Probably the most important example is God's words to the serpent in Genesis 3:15:

> I will put enmity between you and the woman, and between your offspring and hers; he will strike your head, and you will strike his heel.

Originally this passage was a simple reference to ongoing hostility between snakes and people. Humans (collective offspring) will strike at snakes' heads; snakes will strike at human heels.[14] Later Christian theological reflection interpreted the snake as the devil whose defeat seemed to be implied by the contrast between head and heel. Christians understood this passage as a promise of a Savior for humankind; the woman was interpreted to be Mary, and her offspring (singular) was Jesus.

St. Irenaeus of Lyons, writing in the late second century, "unpacked" this verse at length to prove that it was a prophetic reference to Mary and that her "offspring" was Jesus. Through a mistranslation, however, the text Irenaeus worked with said *"she* will strike your head, and you will strike *her* heel." So Irenaeus wrote that Jesus was the Second Adam, who resisted the attacks of the devil, in contrast to the First Adam, who had fallen. On the cross, the devil struck at the Second Adam, who conquered all the same.

Another Old Testament passage received a messianic interpretation from the earliest days of Christianity: "Therefore the Lord himself will give you a sign. Look, the young woman is with child and shall bear a son, and shall name him Immanuel" (Isaiah 7:14). Older Catholic translations rendered the Hebrew word *Ha'almâ* as "virgin." But the Hebrew term for virgin is *betûlâ*.

Although the Christian interpretation of this passage is understandable and theologically legitimate, the original Hebrew reference was, most likely, to a wife of King Ahaz, whose child would save the kingdom of Israel.[15]

CHAPTER TWO

Mary After the New Testament

A s we turn our attention to later Christian reflection on, and interpretation of, Mary, we need to remember not to leave behind the real, historical Mary of Nazareth, the Jewish girl who changed the course of human history by saying yes to God's will for her. For it is her faith that matters most and makes her important to all Christians for all times.

In their earliest decades, Christian communities struggled to survive in the powerful yet declining Roman Empire. There we find no evidence for a unified understanding of Mary and her place in Christian life and faith. In fact, she is rarely mentioned. This may be because the Hellenistic religions of the time almost always had feminine deities, mother-goddesses. When proclaiming the gospel to gentile peoples inclined to belief in goddess cults, the earliest Christian preachers may have wanted to avoid the risk of emphasizing Mary, as this could lead to misinterpretations of her and her role in Christianity.[1]

The earliest mention of Mary outside of documents that became part of the New Testament is in the letters of St. Ignatius, bishop of Antioch, from the late first or early second century. Ignatius died about the year 107. In his Letter to the Ephesians, he mentions three central mysteries of the Christian faith: "Mary's virginity and her giving birth ... and the Lord's death" (19:1).[2] In the same letter, he says that Christ was "sprung from Mary as well as God" (7:2), and "conceived by Mary" (18:2).

In his Letter to the Trallians, Ignatius writes: "Be deaf ... to any talk that ignores Jesus Christ, of David's lineage, [born] of

Mary" (9:1-2). Finally, in his Letter to the Smyrnaeans, Ignatius remarks that Christ was "actually born of a virgin" (1:1).

Ignatius' concise comments about Mary are important because they reflect the fact that Mary's role is important to Ignatius. He includes Mary in early statements of Christian faith, and as a bishop he speaks with special authority.

By the latter half of the second century, however, two ways of understanding Mary emerged, one coming from theological reflection, the other from popular piety.[3]

Mary, the New Eve and Guarantor of the Incarnation

St. Paul described Jesus as the New Adam (Romans 5:14). During the second century, early Christian theologians concluded from this that Mary, the Mother of Jesus, could rightly be called the New Eve. During the first half of the second century, but after Ignatius of Antioch, St. Justin Martyr wrote what is probably the first example of this line of thought:

> For Eve, being a virgin and undefiled, having conceived the word from the serpent, brought forth disobedience and death. The Virgin Mary, however, having received faith and joy, when the angel Gabriel announced to her the good tidings ... answered: Be it done to me according to thy word.[4]

St. Irenaeus, who died in the early second century and was the first great Christian theologian after St. Paul, introduced into Western Christianity some of the deep devotion to Mary found in the East. Whereas Eve was disobedient, Irenaeus said, Mary was obedient and in her obedience she canceled Eve's sin. Perhaps more significantly, Irenaeus declared that Mary can intercede for us with God. But Irenaeus did feel free to criticize Mary for, in effect, getting pushy with her son at the wedding at Cana, pressuring him to reveal himself before he was ready to do so.[5]

Irenaeus saw Mary as quite human, much like any mother. But it is precisely because he took Mary's humanity seriously that Irenaeus was able to situate Mary at the center of the drama of redemption. He called her "the pure womb which regenerates men unto God."[6]

Tertullian, one of the most influential of the early fathers of the church, was bishop of Carthage and died about the year 220. Tertullian wanted to avoid comparisons between Mary and the Egyptian goddess Isis. He also was concerned about Gnostic Christians who tended not to take Christ's humanity seriously enough. Because of such issues, Tertullian went out of his way to describe Mary in simple, human terms.

In some ways Tertullian's assessment of Mary seems rather severe. For example, he did not believe that Mary was among her son's followers. Instead, he tended to align Mary with antagonistic elements in the Jewish community. Tertullian wrote that Jesus spurned his mother and "transferred the blessedness from the womb and breasts of his mother to his disciples."[7]

Even so, Tertullian wrote that Mary's obedience to God was her greatest virtue. He may well have wanted to hold up Mary as an example to the women of his time, as an inspiration to them to be obedient to their husbands and other male authority figures. In this, Tertullian was simply a man of his time and culture.

The Mary of Popular Devotion
Other developments in Marian theology unfolded on the level

of ordinary, pious believers, but they were no less influential than what came from theologians.

One Marian hymn in what may be the earliest Christian hymnbook, written in Syriac, includes this description of Mary giving birth to Jesus:

> She brought forth like a strong man with desire,
> And she bore according to the manifestation
> And acquired with great power.[8]

According to the translator of these lines, James Hamilton Charlesworth, this Marian hymn would have been used in Christian worship services during the second century.[9]

As for visual portrayals of Mary, as early as A.D. 150, a fresco of the Virgin and Child was painted in the catacomb of Priscilla, in Rome.[10]

The Juggler of God

In the Middle Ages many legends about Mary and the child Jesus were told or sung or dramatized. One is the famous French legend of the juggler of God. In this story, a boy spends his life juggling colored balls to entertain people, and always the last ball added to the many he juggled is a golden ball, which he calls "the sun in the sky."

As an old man, the juggler is no longer popular, and the crowds ridicule him when he tries to entertain them with his juggling. He finds his way to a monastery where a procession to honor the Virgin and Child is in progress, all the people

Perhaps the most remarkable popular document about Mary that emerged in the first centuries of the church was the Infancy Gospel of James.[11] Written about the same time as documents that were included in the New Testament, the Infancy Gospel of James is filled with legends, some charming fantasies, others purporting to be factual. It also owes more than a little to the Old Testament story of Abraham and Sarah, who had a child in old age (Genesis 17:15ff).

The Infancy Gospel of James says that Mary was a virgin not only in the conception of Jesus, but that she also miraculously and literally remained a virgin, her hymen intact, after giving birth. It also says that Mary experienced no discomfort or pain as she gave birth, and it hypothesizes that the "brothers of Jesus" spoken of in the Gospels were children of Joseph from a first marriage. This document never became a part of the New Testament, yet it influenced the development of Marian

---

bringing gifts to lay before a statue of the Virgin and Child. After all the people depart, the old juggler kneels before the statue. He notices that the Child seems unhappy. He tells the Virgin and Child that he has nothing to offer except his juggling. So he begins, his colored balls flying in the air. As always, the last ball added to the several he keeps in midair is the golden ball, "the sun in the sky."

The next morning, two monks discover the body of the old juggler, dead in front of the statue of the Virgin and Child. The monks gasp. The Child has a smile on his face, and in his hands he holds the golden ball.[12]

legends, some of which some believers mistake as factual and a part of Catholic doctrine.[13]

There are grounds to suppose that some of these legends about the Virgin Mary may implicitly have represented a hesitancy to ascribe total humanity to her divine Son, as that hesitancy was already being expressed in other sources written about the same time.[14]

The following is a summary of the Infancy Gospel of James.

The document begins by introducing a wealthy, kind, and generous older couple, Joachim and Anne, who have no children. As the "great day of the Lord" draws near, someone named Reubel informs Joachim that, being childless, he may not offer gifts to the Lord. A distressed Joachim goes off into the wilderness, sets up a tent, and fasts for forty days, "until the Lord God visits me. Prayer will be my food and drink."

Because Joachim did not tell Anne where he was going, she assumes he has died and mourns both him and the child she never had. But an angel appears to both Anne and Joachim to announce that they will have a child, a gift of God. Anne says that she will dedicate the child to God "its whole life."

Anne births a daughter, named Mary. When the girl is six months old, she takes seven steps, into Anne's arms. Anne immediately says that her daughter's feet will not touch the ground again until she is living in the temple.

On Mary's first birthday, Joachim throws "a great banquet" at which the priests and high priests pronounce blessings on the child. Then Anne takes the baby to a private room to nurse her and sings: "I will sing a sacred song to the Lord my God because he has visited me and taken away the disgrace … ."

When Mary is two, Joachim suggests to Anne that they take Mary to the temple to keep their promise "or else the Lord will be angry with us and our gift will be unacceptable." But Anne isn't ready, suggesting they wait another year, so the girl won't be homesick. Joachim readily agrees.

When Mary is three, Joachim and Anne finally take her to the temple, where the priest welcomes her, kisses her, and blesses her with a prophetic remark with clear connections to Mary's Magnificat in the Gospel of Luke: "The Lord has exalted your name among all generations. In you the Lord will disclose his redemption to the people of Israel during the last days."

The priest places the girl—dedicated to be a virgin—in front of the altar, and God showers favor on her. "She danced, and the whole house of Israel loved her."

Mary lives in the temple, her meals brought to her by heavenly messengers. When she is twelve, however, the priests get nervous knowing that soon Mary will menstruate, which will "pollute the sanctuary of the Lord."

God tells the high priest Zechariah to gather together "the widowers of the people," instructing each to bring with him a staff. "She will become the wife of the one to whom the Lord God shows a sign." Among the widowers is Joseph, who "threw down his carpenter's ax" and joined the gathering.

Zechariah collects all the staffs, prays, then returns them to their owners, Joseph being the last to receive his staff. Suddenly a dove flies from Joseph's staff and perches on his head. Zechariah says this means that Joseph should take Mary into his "care and protection." Joseph isn't so sure. "I already have sons, and I'm an old man; she's only a young woman; I'm afraid that I will become the butt of jokes."

Zechariah reminds Joseph that people who have refused the will of the Lord have suffered for it. Because he is afraid, Joseph takes Mary home with him to care for her, though he tells her that he will be traveling, "to build houses, but I'll come back to you. The Lord will protect you."

One day, at the water well, Mary hears a voice speaking the same words recorded in the Gospel of Luke: "Greetings, favored one! The Lord is with you. Blessed are you among women." Looking around, Mary sees no one, and she runs home terrified. Back home, "a heavenly messenger" appears and tells her not to be afraid. "You have found favor in the sight of the Lord of all. You will conceive by means of his word."

Mary listens but has her doubts. What about the birth itself? she asks. Will it be a normal birth? When the angel says no, Mary responds, "Here I am, the Lord's slave before him. I pray that all you've told me comes true."

Mary visits her relative Elizabeth, but the account here in the Infancy Gospel of James adds a human dimension to the story that is missing from Luke's version. Mary stays with Elizabeth for three months. "And day by day her womb kept swelling." Amazing as it may seem, Mary forgets what the angel Gabriel—here named for the first time—previously has told her, and she is frightened by the changes in her body.

Mary returns home and hides. The Infancy Gospel of James says that Mary is now sixteen, which would mean she has been "in Joseph's care" for four years. Three months later Joseph comes home from work and sees that Mary is pregnant. His response is much more human than that recorded in the Gospel of Matthew: "He struck himself in the face, threw himself to the ground on sackcloth, and began to cry bitterly."

"Who has lured this virgin away from me and violated her?" Joseph cries. How could Mary have done such an awful thing after being chosen by the Lord and raised in the temple? She wails and claims her innocence. "I haven't had sex with any man."

Joseph remains unconvinced. How did Mary get pregnant? Mary's response confirms that she has forgotten the visit from Gabriel: "As the Lord my God lives, I don't know where [the child] came from."

Unlike the account in Matthew's Gospel, here we are privy to Joseph's inner reasoning. Terrified, Joseph thinks through his options. He could "cover up her sin," but that would violate Jewish law. He could "disclose her condition" publicly, but if the child was "heaven-sent" he would cause an innocent death. Feeling both options unacceptable, he says he will instead "divorce her quietly."

In the next scene, Annas, a "scholar," visits Joseph and notices that Mary is pregnant. He quickly leaves and reports the situation to the high priest, who calls in Mary and Joseph and accuses Mary: "Why have you humiliated yourself?"

But Mary defends herself. She has not been with any man.

Then the priest accuses Joseph, who defends himself. "I am innocent where she is concerned." But the priest does not believe Joseph and again accuses him of fathering the child.

Joseph remains silent, and the high priest orders him to return Mary to the temple. At this, Joseph starts crying. So the priest agrees to give Joseph "the Lord's drink test," which will reveal the guilt of both Joseph and Mary. It's not clear how this test works, but Joseph must drink special water and go "into the wilderness," from which he returns safely. Then Mary takes the same test, also returning unharmed, which proved their innocence, to the surprise of all.

The high priest therefore does not condemn the couple but

dismisses Joseph and Mary, who return home, "praising the God of Israel."

From here on, the author of the Infancy Gospel of James blends the narratives of Matthew and Luke into one story, giving the perspectives of both Joseph and Mary. We also get a few original bits of dialogue. "Joseph, help me down from the donkey," Mary says, explaining that her time is at hand. Joseph replies: "Where will I take you to give you some privacy … ?"

Locating a cave, Joseph takes Mary inside, and now we learn that they have traveling companions. "He stationed his sons to guard her and went to look for a Hebrew midwife" near

Grimm's Tales

The famous Brothers Grimm, Jacob (1785–1863) and Wilhelm (1786–1859), in their *Fairy Tales*, included a story titled "The Child of Mary." This story is about the daughter of a poor woodcutter whom Mary befriends and takes with her to heaven. Mary leaves on a journey, but not before telling the girl not to open a certain door. Of course, the girl cannot resist. When she opens the door in Mary's absence, the girl sees the Holy Trinity seated in flaming glory.

When Mary returns, the girl will not acknowledge her disobedience, so Mary banishes her from heaven. The girl becomes unable to speak and barely manages to survive, living in a dark and forbidding forest. One day, however, the local king goes hunting in the forest, discovers the girl, takes her back to his castle, and marries her. Later, when the young queen—still speechless—is about to give birth, Mary appears and again asks her to admit her disobedience. But the young woman refuses, so Mary takes the baby from her. Everyone thinks the silent queen has killed her baby.

Bethlehem. Notice, there is no mention of using the cave because there was "no room in the inn," an element of Luke's account that the James author apparently thought unimportant.

That night, consistent with Matthew's narrative, Joseph has a dream, an angel saying not to be afraid, that Mary's pregnancy has divine origins, and Joseph is to name the child Jesus. Joseph gets up and praises God and begins "to protect the girl."

Describing Joseph walking in the countryside, looking for a midwife, the narrative reads like science fiction. Everything Joseph sees has stopped moving. Clouds are motionless in the sky. Shepherds and their sheep are frozen in time. Birds are sus-

---

The same sequence of events repeats itself the following year, but the king intervenes to protect his wife from the angry crowd. The third year the same thing happens again, but this time the king cannot protect her, and she is condemned—to be burned at the stake. Facing the flames, the queen repents of her guilt and calls out in her heart—still being unable to speak—"Yes, Mary, I did it!" Immediately, a rain storm extinguishes the fire, and Mary appears, bringing back the three children. She also returns to the queen the gift of speech.

The Brothers Grimm also wrote a tale called "The Little Glass of the Mother of God." In this story, Mary asks a poor coachman to give her a glass of wine, but the man has no glass. Mary picks a flower which, by a miracle, she can use as a glass. Ever since, this flower has been called "the little glass of the Mother of God."

In yet another Brothers Grimm story, Mary is looking for strawberries for the boy Jesus. A snake bites Jesus, who hides behind a hazel shrub. Ever since, this shrub is thought to be a sure protection against snakes and other dangers.[15]

pended in midair. Then suddenly everything starts moving again.

Joseph encounters a woman who asks him what he is looking for. "A Hebrew midwife." She—a midwife herself—accompanies Joseph to the cave, listening to his explanation, that Mary is about to have a baby conceived by the Holy Spirit. When they reach the cave, it is overshadowed by a dark cloud. Suddenly, however, the cloud vanishes, replaced by a light so bright they can't bear to look at it. When the light dims, Joseph and the midwife discover Mary with the infant Jesus at her breast.

Amazed and shocked, the midwife leaves and encounters a new character, Salome, who refuses to believe when the midwife tells her that a virgin has given birth. Reminiscent of the story of the apostle Thomas, who doubted that Jesus had risen from the dead (see John 20:24-28), Salome declares that she will not believe "unless I insert my finger and examine her."

Salome and the midwife return to the cave, and the midwife tells Mary she must allow herself to be examined. "You are facing a serious test." So Mary "positioned herself," and Salome discovers the hymen intact. Salome is horrified: "because of my transgression and my disbelief, I have put the living God on trial!" Before her very eyes her hand starts to disappear, "being consumed by flames!"

An angel again appears and directs Salome to pick up the child, which she does and is instantly healed. The Infancy Gospel of James now concludes with its own version of the visit from the Magi and the murder of children by Herod searching for the infant Messiah. But James includes an original account of Elizabeth escaping with the infant John the Baptist and the murder of Elizabeth's husband, Zechariah, by Herod's soldiers.

Commenting on apocryphal accounts such as the Infancy Gospel of James, Sally Cunneen points out how remarkable it is that in a first-century male-dominated society, ordinary Christians imagined Mary to be remarkably strong and independent:

> They imagined her life to be almost angelic, but at the same time they made her humanly accessible and provided her with an extended family not mentioned in the New Testament. Mary and Joseph became leading characters in legends composed by Christians in Syria, by Egyptian farmers, and by sailors of the Nile who carried them as far as Arabia. These fictional inventions supplied imaginative details and dialogue for what the Gospels left out.[16]

During the centuries that followed, Marian legends spread throughout the Christian world. The Christian imagination, it seems, could not get enough of Mary. Later apocryphal tales included stories about the escape of Joseph, Mary, and the infant Jesus into Egypt.

CHAPTER THREE

Mary Throughout History

During the early decades of the Christian era, believers blended New Testament images of Mary so that they supported one another and formed a unified image in the popular imagination. The woman of faith (Luke-Acts), the Virgin who gave birth to the Messiah (Matthew), and the Mother who stood at the foot of the cross (John) became one image in the minds of Christians.

This image merged with the popular interpretation of the "woman clothed with the sun" from the Book of Revelation (intended by the author to be an image of the church, the new Israel) and the apocryphal Mary in the Infancy Gospel of James. This latter source added to the mix a legendary account of Mary's family background, childhood, and engagement and marriage to Joseph. So the Mary present in the popular imagination by the middle of the third century is all of these images rolled into one.

In the third and fourth centuries, the tradition of writing hymns to Mary was firmly established. One of the oldest Marian lyrics was discovered on a papyrus from this era. A prayer to Mary, it acknowledges that "we flee" to Mary for protection. The prayer-hymn ends:

> Lead us to your Son,
> recommend us to your Son,
> present us to your Son.[1]

Notice that early Christians evidently realized that it was critical to maintain the priority of Christ over Mary. Mary receives honor and acclaim, but she is not about to become a substitute for Christ.

Perhaps the first example of a Marian hymn attributed to a named author is by St. Gregory the Wonderworker, a convert who became a student of Origen (d. 254), "the greatest scholar and most prolific author of the early church."[2] Gregory became bishop of Neocaesarea and died about the year 275. The hymn, addressed to Mary, has a clear trinitarian theme, saying that in Mary

> is the Father glorified ...
> is the Son adored ...
> is the Holy Spirit celebrated.[3]

Devotional writers from the earliest days of the church had no reservations when it came to composing hymns, poems, and other literary works about and addressed to Mary. This early literature gives witness to the great affection Christians felt for the Mother of the Lord. Clearly these early followers of Christ saw no reason that Christ's being the one Mediator between God and humankind should mean less devotion to the woman chosen by God to bring the Son of God into human history.

Turning to the theological, scholarly writings of the first two or three centuries of the church, we find little emphasis on Mary. As we saw in chapter 2, however, three themes did emerge during this period. Mary was seen as the New Eve, who, by her obedience to God, canceled out the disobedience of the first Eve. Through disobedience the first Eve brought death into the world; by obedience Mary brought life into the world, specifically new life in Christ. Mary's virginity in both conceiving and giving birth to Jesus was seen as perpetual, and the early fathers of the church believed this was attested to by Scripture. Finally, Jesus being the Word (second Person of the Trinity) incarnate, made flesh, meant that Mary was truly the Mother of God: *Theotokos*, in Greek, or God-bearer. ("In the beginning was the Word, and the Word was with God, and the Word was God.... And the Word became flesh and lived among us" [John 1:1, 14].)

St. Augustine (d. 430) contemplated the mystery of the Incarnation using bridal imagery:

> How could you have merited that your maker should take form in you? That the Word of God by whom you were made and by whom even heaven and earth and all things were made, should take flesh in you, making flesh his own without losing his divinity? The Word is joined to flesh; the Word is married to flesh, and your womb is the bridal chamber of that great marriage.[4]

St. Ambrose (d. 397) and St. Augustine saw Mary as a symbol of the church, which is known as the bride of Christ (Revelation 22:17). In the following centuries, Mary takes on significance as being both the Mother and the Bride of God.

Mother of God

In the fifth century, the traditional belief in Mary as *Theotokos*, God-bearer or Mother of God, became the center of an intense theological controversy. The dispute was about Christ, however, not Mary. Nestorius, the bishop and patriarch of Constantinople, declared that Christ had two distinct natures, one human, the other divine, and the divine nature was contained within the human nature. Therefore it was proper to say that Mary was the Mother of Christ, but not the Mother of God. On the contrary, declared the Council of Ephesus in 431. There was only one divine Person in Christ, fully human and fully divine. This meant it was perfectly accurate to say that Mary was the Mother of God (*Theotokos*).

The official document issued by the Council of Ephesus says:

We confess, therefore, our Lord Jesus Christ, the only-begotten Son of God, perfect God and perfect Man, consisting of a rational soul and a body begotten of the Father before the ages as touching his Godhead, the same, in the last days, for us and for our salvation, born of the Virgin Mary, as touching his Manhood; the same of one substance with us as touching his Manhood. For of two natures a union has been made. For this cause we confess one Christ, one Son, one Lord.

In accordance with this sense of the unconfused union, we confess the holy Virgin to be *Theotokos,* because God the Word became incarnate and was made man, and from the very conception united to himself the temple taken from her....[5]

The proclamation is ultimately about Jesus, but it did result in encouraging devotion to Mary. By "devotion to" we mean simply an affection for Mary and a prayerful spirit that includes her—in a subservient way, of course—in one's faith relationship with Christ.

Mary as Intercessor

The image of Mary as mediatrix (feminine form of mediator) of God's grace became more and more prominent. Mediatrix was first used of Mary in the sixth century. This title simply means that being "so close to her Son, Mary can intercede for her other children (John 19:26), an intercession that relies on her Son's infinite merits."[6]

An influential hymn to Mary, called the *Akathistos,* probably originated in the East in the sixth century. This hymn celebrates Mary's role as *Theotokos:*

Hail, you who carried in your womb
The guide for all who stray....[7]

The *Akathistos* portrays Mary as "the receptacle of wisdom, mighty intercessor, and minister of divine goodness."[8] This hymn had a tremendous impact on the church, implying that Mary has divine powers. In fact, Christians began to take the words of this hymn, and others like it, literally, which influenced the development of the Marian theological tradition in unbalanced ways.

Note this prayer to Mary, written by St. Germanus (d. 733) of Constantinople, which shows great regard to Mary and her power; it also shows the mix of mother and bridal imagery:

My Lady, my refuge, life, and help, my armor and my boast, my hope and my strength, grant that I may enjoy the ineffable, inconceivable gifts of your Son, your God and our God. For I know surely that you have power to do as you will, since you are Mother of the Most High.... O Spouse of God, who bore him who is the expectation of all....[9]

By the Middle Ages, Marian devotion sometimes took on inappropriate proportions. The belief developed that Mary had a mother's influence with God and that she could deflect Christ's just anger and gain mercy for poor sinners. Mary became the kind, gentle intercessor who could change her stern son's mind, sometimes even manipulating him to get her way. This idea was highly influential in the East, as witnessed by the popularity of the Theophilus legend.

This story tells of a man named Theophilus who agrees to let the devil have his soul (at death) in exchange for a high-paying position. But as he nears death, Theophilus pleads with Mary to help him by getting back the contract he foolishly signed with the devil. Mary confronts the devil and gets back the contract, and Theophilus dies in peace, escaping the everlasting flames of hell.

The Theophilus legend was translated from Greek into Latin in the 900s and had great influence on the church in the West and the understanding in Western spirituality of Mary's power to help those who prayed to her. (The Eastern—Orthodox—church and the Western—Roman—church did not really split until "the Great Schism" in 1054.) A theological principle even developed saying that God *could* give Mary certain gifts, that he *should* do so, and therefore he *did* so. This principle had a significant impact on theological reflection on Mary during the Middle Ages. Religious thinkers called Mary the channel through which grace flowed from heaven to earth, and the neck between the Head (Christ) and the body of Christ, the church. Some called Mary "the mediator with the Mediator."[10]

Titles were applied to Mary, such as Mother of Mercy and Refuge of Sinners. Mary was easy to turn to because of her maternal love.

Mary as Model of Virginity

For many centuries, the virginity of Mary served as an ideal that motivated countless women, in part at least, to become nuns by emulating Mary's virginity as essential to a woman's total dedication of herself to Christ. During the tenth century, highly influential apocryphal biographies of Mary were written, notably the *Historia nativitatis Dei genitricis,* by Roswitha of Gandersheim, a Benedictine nun and scholar. The main theme of her work was Mary's perpetual virginity. In her story, which by modern standards is fanciful in the extreme, Mary refuses to marry a temple priest on the grounds that she wants to preserve her virginity.[11]

The Assumption of Mary

One of the sixth-century fathers of the church, St. Gregory of Tours (d. 594), building on theological reflection that went back to at least the fourth century, wrote an account of the death of Mary:

> Finally, when blessed Mary, having completed the course of her earthly life, was about to be called from this world, all the apostles, coming from their different regions, gathered together in her house. When they heard that she was about to be taken up out of the world, they kept watch together with her.
>
> And behold, the Lord Jesus came with his angels and, taking her soul, handed it over to the archangel Michael and withdrew. At dawn, the apostles lifted up her body on a pallet, laid it in a tomb, and kept watch over it, awaiting the coming of the Lord. And behold, again the Lord presented himself to them and ordered that her holy body be taken and

carried up to heaven. There she is now, joined once more to her soul; she exults with the elect, rejoicing in the eternal blessings that will have no end.[12]

Though he does not use the word, this is an early account of what is now called the Assumption of Mary—that at the end of her life she was taken into heaven body and soul.

In a document titled *The Dormition [Sleep] of Mary,* St. Modestus of Jerusalem (d. 630) describes the Assumption in poetic terms, describing Mary as the Ark of the New Covenant. "The ark was not drawn by oxen like the Mosaic ark of old, but guided and guarded by a heavenly army of holy angels." He also introduces imagery of Mary as Queen of Heaven.

Because she was his most holy Mother, he bestowed on her the highest honor by making her his heir: as the Psalmist sings: *The Queen stands on your right robed in raiment wrought with gold and diverse colors.*[13]

Belief in the doctrine of the Assumption resulted mainly from preaching and devotional writing. It was thought that in view of her role in the history of salvation, as the Mother of God, it would have been appropriate that she experience death but not bodily decomposition. Through her body Mary gave a human body to Christ, therefore it was appropriate that he see to it that her body know eternal life.

During the Middle Ages, in the West, sermons and devotional literature made routine reference to Christ's respect for his mother, the idea being that he would have obeyed the fourth commandment requiring honor for one's parents. There was also popular repugnance at the notion that the body of the woman who gave birth to the Savior would be allowed to decompose. Therefore, after the thirteenth century, theologians left little doubt that the Assumption actually happened.

Since 1950 the Assumption of Mary is an official dogma of the Catholic faith. (See further discussion in chapters 5 and 6.) There are two traditions regarding where Mary died. "The discrepancies between the stories would alone reflect the absence of a solid historical tradition," says Marina Warner. Early apoc-

---

Song to Mary

St. Hildegard of Bingen (d. 1179), known as a visionary, musician, abbess, and politician, wrote a song to Mary. The first half addresses Mary directly, then the song talks about her, not to her:

O most splendid Gem! The serene beauty of the sun is poured into you, the Fountain springing from the heart of the Father, which is the only begotten Word, through whom he created the primary material of the world, which Eve troubled: He made this Word Man in you, and you are that brilliant Gem, from whom that Word brought forth all the virtues and in that primary matter produced all creatures.

O sweetest Rod, bringing forth leaves from the root of Jesse. Oh, how great is the virtue the Divinity saw in this most beautiful daughter, as an eagle fixes his eye upon the sun, when the Father above regarded the excellency of the Virgin, when he willed that his Word should be incarnate in her. For the soul of the Virgin being illuminated in a hidden mystery of God, the bright Flower issued from this same Virgin in a wonderful way.[14]

ryphal writings indicate she died in Jerusalem, the disciples miraculously being summoned from around the world to her bedside. Yet "none of the early travelers to the Holy Land mention" her grave in Jerusalem. This gives more credence to her assumption—that she has no grave. Some scholars claim Mary died in Ephesus, "where she lived in John's care after the Crucifixion."[15]

Queen of Heaven

The title Queen of Heaven emphasizes Mary's role as queenly intercessor. Because she is *Theotokos* (God-bearer, Mother of God), Mary is Queen of the kingdom of God. Although not included among Catholic dogmas, the coronation of Mary as Queen of Heaven is one of the Glorious Mysteries of the Rosary rooted in early Christian theological reflection that crystallized in the writings of Andrew of Crete (d. ca. 740). In homilies Andrew described Mary as "Queen of the human race," "Immaculate Queen," "Queen of all people," and "New Queen." Andrew wrote: "Queen of the whole human race, truly faithful to the meaning of your name, you are above all things—except God!"[16]

A hymn written in the eleventh century and still popular to this day describes Mary as Queen and pleads for her help. It is known by its Latin name, Salve Regina, or Hail, Holy Queen.

Hail, holy Queen, Mother of Mercy;
Hail our life, our sweetness, and our hope.
To you do we cry, poor banished children of Eve.
To you do we send up our sighs,
Mourning and weeping in this valley of tears.
Turn then, most gracious advocate,

Your eyes of mercy toward us.

And after this our exile,

Show unto us the blessed fruit of your womb, Jesus.

O clement [merciful], O loving, O sweet Virgin Mary.

Pray for us, O holy Mother of God,

That we may become worthy of the promises of Christ.

Some say this song-prayer was written by Adhemar, bishop of Le Puy (d. 1098), but the author may more likely be a German monk, Herman the Lame (d. 1054),

who was born so deformed that he could never stand.... He was a genius who wrote a number of scientific studies, even though his speech was so impaired that he was difficult to understand. Herman eventually went blind and turned his talent to writing hymns and poems. The Salve Regina ... has been recited billions of times since his death, bringing hope and joy to those who prayed it in dark times.[17]

Hundreds of legends about Mary developed during the Middle Ages. Mary appears in all kinds of situations, but all of them end with her being crowned Queen of Heaven. In one legend, a thief has a deep devotion to Mary. The thief is caught and hanged for his crimes, but he hangs on the gallows for three days feeling no pain at all, and he senses that Mary is supporting him and keeping him from death. When the executioners find the thief still alive, they assume the hanging was not done correctly, so they try to behead him. Mary prevents the headsman from decapitating the thief, however, and the thief goes free.

These legends always depict Mary as "the kind, forgiving

helper of the poor, the oppressed, and sinners."[18] Mary always prefers mercy to justice, no matter what the situation.

The Immaculate Conception

There is no early explicit reference to what is now known as the Immaculate Conception—the belief that Mary herself was free from original sin from the moment of her conception in her mother's womb. Yet reflection on Mary as the New Eve prepared the way for this belief. By the eleventh century, traditions regarding Mary's special holiness and the unique nature of her own conception came together in England where a feast of the Immaculate Conception emerged.

Eadmer of Canterbury (d. 1124) wrote a *Tract on the Conception of Mary*, which first lays out the doctrine of the Immaculate Conception. Addressing Mary, he wrote that God "willed to make you his Mother." After more description, he continued: "It was for this destiny that he formed you by the action of the Holy Spirit, in the womb of your mother, from the very first instant of your conception...."[19]

Opposition to the English feast day celebrating the Immaculate Conception led to the earliest theological examination of this belief. The main theological objection to the Immaculate Conception surfaced during the twelfth and thirteenth centuries. If Mary herself was conceived in her mother's womb without being affected by original sin, some theologians asked, does this not mean that she had no need for salvation like the rest of humankind? Ultimately the response was that salvation can happen in two ways. Christ can save those already in sin, and he can save by preserving someone from being touched by sin at all. Mary is the sole example of the second option.

Mary as Rose

Mary, of course, has come to be associated with rosary beads and a prayer known as the Rosary. Traditionally Mary herself has been referred to as a Rose. The word *rosary* comes from the Latin, *rosarium,* meaning rose garden. The connection between the "rose garden" image and Mary can be traced to the Song of Songs in the Old Testament. There the bride is described as "a rose of Sharon, a lily of the valleys" (2:1). The Song of Songs was written as a celebration of erotic love, and this meaning remains valid. Interpreted from a Christian perspective, however, it also symbolizes the passionate love between Christ and his people, the church, the woman representing the church, again, the bride of Christ.

Star of the Sea

St. Bernard of Clairvaux (d. 1153), a founder of the Trappists (Order of Cistercians of the Strict Observance), wrote many Marian poems and hymns and used imaginative imagery in describing her. For example, he compared her to an aqueduct that carries God's grace to the faithful. He also compared Mary to the fragrance of fruit that remains on one's hand after the fruit is consumed.

In a commentary on the name of Mary, Bernard wrote that the name means Star of the Sea. "Just as the star sends out rays without being damaged, so the Virgin gives birth unimpaired.... She sparkles through her good deeds, she shines through her good example.... When the winds of temptation arise, when you run into the cliff of affliction, look up to the star, call on Mary."[20]

Medieval commentators saw Mary as the woman in the Song of Songs, and the garden in which she dwells was the "rose garden" of Mary.[21] Later, in the writings of the twelfth-century mystic and monastic reformer St. Bernard of Clairvaux (d. 1153), the rose became a symbol for Mary herself. (See further discussion of the Rosary in chapter 7.)

Mother of the Church

In chapter 1 we discussed how Jesus' crucifixion conversation with his disciple John laid the foundation for Mary being seen as Mother of the Church. The title was first used in the eighth century.[22]

Through the Middle Ages, the concept of Mary as the believer's Mother sometimes took on graphic interpretations. Marina Warner notes,

> The association of Mary's milk with her powers of intercession and healing inspired an extraordinary quantity of relics in Europe. From the thirteenth century, phials in which her milk was preserved were venerated all over Christendom in shrines that attracted pilgrims by the thousands.... Sometimes the relic purported to be a piece of the ground of the grotto at Bethlehem where a few drops had spilt while Mary was nursing. This place, known as the Milk Grotto, can still be visited by tourists to the Holy Land.[23]

Mother of Sorrows

The veneration of Mary as the Mother of Sorrows (*Mater Dolorosa*) spread across Europe in the eleventh century. St. Bernard claimed that Mary was martyred, in spirit not in body. St. Francis of Assisi (d. 1226) introduced theological drama, reenacting biblical scenes. The stations of the cross became popular, sometimes highlighting Mary's suffering nearly as much as Jesus'.

The Stabat Mater (Sorrowful Mother), a thirteenth-century prayer-hymn—here in a nineteenth-century translation—typifies Mary as the great suffering Mother:

> At the cross her station keeping,
> Stood the mournful Mother weeping,
> Where he hung, the dying Lord:
> For her soul of joy bereaved,
> Bowed with anguish deeply grieved,
> Felt the sharp and piercing sword.
>
> Who, on Christ's dear Mother gazing,
> Pierced by anguish so amazing,
> Born of woman, would not weep?
> Who, on Christ's dear Mother thinking,
> Such a cup of sorrow drinking,
> Would not share her sorrows deep?
>
> Jesus, may her deep devotion
> Stir in me the same emotion,
> Fount of love, Redeemer kind;
> That my heart fresh ardor gaining,
> And a purer love attaining,
> May with thee acceptance find.

The Black Plague, which swept Europe in the fourteenth century, was seen by many as punishment from an angry God. Mary, the compassionate, suffering Mother, served as a great comforter in distress.

Devotional Excesses

In the Middle Ages, many people expressed their affection for Mary by making pilgrimages to Marian devotional sites all over Europe. Jesus became more and more distant from the lives of ordinary people; when he did appear, he was portrayed as a far-removed Judge. Instead, they venerated images of Mary and attended dramatic reenactments of miracles and apparitions attributed to her.

A reaction to the inflated devotion to Mary was bound to come, and it did during the Protestant Reformation, in the mid-sixteenth century. The reformers themselves spoke favorably of an appropriate devotion to Mary. Martin Luther called Mary "the workshop of God." He said that praise for Mary should not be founded on the virtues of Mary herself but upon the graces given to her by God. John Calvin said, "We cannot celebrate the blessings given us in Christ without commemorating at the same time how high an honor God has granted to Mary when He chose to make her the Mother of His only Son." Huldreich Zwingli recommended praying the Hail Mary, saying, "The more honor and love for Christ, the more also the esteem and honor for Mary."[24]

It didn't take long, however, before Protestants in general wanted nothing to do with devotion to Mary. Responding to the Reformation, the pope called for what is now called the Council of Trent (1545–63). The council's responses to other aspects of the Protestant Reformation were strong and sharp, but its response to the Reformation's criticism of devotion to Mary was low key, recommending proper and useful prayer for the intercession of the saints and asking bishops to be vigilant concerning devotional abuses.

After Trent

During the centuries that followed the Council of Trent, devotion to Mary virtually disappeared among Protestant Christians, while it continued to develop in Catholicism. The seventeenth century, particularly in France, saw an intense period of devotion to Mary. Authors such as Pierre de Bérulle, Jean-Jacques Olier, St. John Eudes (d. 1680), and St. Louis-Marie Grignion de Montfort (d. 1716) contributed to an understanding of Marian devotion that influenced Catholics well into the twentieth century. Today, however, their Marian spirituality strikes many Catholics as sentimental and exaggerated. For example, de Montfort wrote that *True Devotion to the Blessed Virgin* (the title of his book) "sweetens and makes easy the difficult road to union with God."[25] He also declared that one not only could, but *must*, go through Mary to reach Christ. For de Montfort, Mary's influence is so great that she has power even over God.

In Spain, Blessed Mary of Agreda (d. 1665) wrote a huge, very popular tome titled *Mystical City of God*, "an extended 'life of Mary' based on visions and voices and, she admitted, a bit of imagined embellishment."[26]

The Enlightenment of the eighteenth century emphasized rationalism, which lent little support to this sort of romantic, sentimental devotion to Mary. The nineteenth century, however, was characterized by romanticism, and this led to another period of increasing devotion to Mary, which we will discuss in chapter five.

CHAPTER FOUR

Marian Apparitions

It is hard to understand the devotion to Mary of the nineteenth and early twentieth centuries without having some awareness of the Marian apparitions that generated great popular interest in those periods.

Since the Middle Ages, there have been many reports of apparitions, or appearances, of Mary. Benedict Groeschel defines *apparition,* saying it "simply means an occasion when a presumably sane and sincere person reports 'seeing and hearing' a heavenly visitor, usually the Blessed Virgin Mary...."[1]

Accounts of Marian apparitions have always been a challenge to church leaders, who must try to discern whether each reported apparition is authentic. The church's official position on such apparition sites is, first, to reserve judgment. In the modern era, the local bishop investigates each claim and often appoints a commission to investigate. Some apparitions have been recognized by the church as authentic, but many more have been judged undecided or rejected, possibly the result of religious hysteria or outright fraud.

Official approval says that the apparitions support the genuine spirit of the gospel, which is always the ultimate standard. It is entirely up to the individual believer to include or exclude devotion based on apparitions. Even when the church announces that a given apparition is genuine, however, no Catholic is obliged to believe in its authenticity. "Approval" of an apparition simply means that the church does not think that belief in the apparition is phony or harmful, and it may be helpful to one's faith.

Seven Marian apparitions have been given some form of recognition by church authorities.[2]

In describing these apparitions, Pamela Moran notes:

Mary's appearances share some striking similarities. First, she does not come to the wealthy or learned among us, but rather to the poorest, humblest, most unlearned of her children—to those who would receive her message simply and without question. Second, her message is always the same: Mary calls us to repent of our disobedience to God, to return to a life of prayer and penance, a life of faith and love. Third, to convince us of God's love and mercy, Mary brings his healing to many.[3]

Now we will take a look at five of the most popular of these officially approved apparitions, in chronological order.

Our Lady of Guadalupe

The well-known story of Our Lady of Guadalupe is verified by historical research.[4] Early in the morning of December 9, 1531, a fifty-seven-year-old Aztec Indian peasant named Juan Diego, a recent convert to Christianity, was on his way to Mass. As he crossed the hill called Tepeyac, outside Mexico City—the site of an ancient temple of Tonantzin, virgin mother of the old Aztec gods—suddenly he saw a beautiful young woman who appeared to be pregnant. The woman spoke to Juan Diego in his own Aztec language: "Know and understand that I am the ever-virgin Holy Mary, mother of the true God, from whom one lives; the Creator, the Lord of Near and Togetherness, the Lord of Heaven and Earth." Later, in subsequent appearances, the woman called herself "Our Lady of Guadalupe," although

"Guadalupe" could be an adapted Spanish form of the Aztec word Juan Diego actually used.

The holy lady gave Juan Diego a message for the bishop: "I ardently desire that a shrine may be built on this site, so that in it I can give all my love, compassion, help, and protection; for I am your most holy mother, ready to hear all your laments and to alleviate all your miseries, pains, and sufferings."

As a sign of authenticity for the bishop, the lady caused roses to bloom on Tepeyac in December. She directed Juan Diego to fill his tilma, or cloak, with roses for the bishop. Later, when the peasant opened his cloak to give the roses to the bishop, out tumbled the flowers, and miraculously imprinted on his tilma was a picture of the lady herself. The picture is of a young Aztec woman, apparently pregnant.

At some later time, piety led an artist to tamper with the tilma, adding a gold border and gold stars to the lady's garments, plus a sunburst background, and under her feet a cherub angel and a crescent moon. These well-meant touches show signs of deterioration today, but the original image does not. Powerful magnification reveals in the eyes of the holy lady images of the first people who saw her picture on the tilma. The garment is woven from cactus fibers that normally would fall apart in twenty years. This miraculous tilma remains intact more than four hundred years later, displayed in the cathedral of Our Lady of Guadalupe, in Mexico City.

Our Lady of Guadalupe became a powerful symbol for the native peoples of Mexico that made it possible for them to accept Christianity. Even today, she is a symbol of liberation, with tremendous influence on the Latin American imagination, which is why Hispanic people celebrate this memorial with great festivity.

In 1979 Pope John Paul II chose for his first international trip as pope a visit to Mexico, "to invoke on my pontificate the motherly protection and assistance of Our Lady of Guadalupe...."[5] In 1998 Pope John Paul II beatified Juan Diego, the next-to-last step toward canonization as a saint.

Our Lady of the Miraculous Medal

Three hundred years after the apparitions in Mexico, Mary appeared to an obscure French nun named Catherine Labouré (1806–76). Born Zoé Labouré, Sister Catherine was a poorly educated peasant who entered the Sisters of Charity of St. Vincent de Paul in 1830 and moved to Paris. She lived in a convent on the Rue du Bac. On July 18, 1830, it is said that the Blessed Virgin Mary appeared to Sister Catherine for several hours while she was at prayer in the convent chapel. Again on November 27, Mary appeared to Sister Catherine and instructed her to have a medal designed that would represent Mary as Catherine had seen her.

Subsequently, this medal was reproduced almost endlessly, and it came to be known as the Miraculous Medal. On the medal, Mary stands on a half-globe. Rays of light stream from her fingers, and words appear around her figure: "O Mary conceived without sin, pray for us who have recourse to thee."

Mary appeared to Sister Catherine several more times until September 1831. The nun's confessor, Father Aladel, promoted devotion to the Miraculous Medal, but Sister Catherine herself remained virtually unknown until after her death. She was canonized a saint in 1947, and her feast day is December 30.

Our Lady of La Salette

On September 19, 1846, two young French peasants, Melanie Mathieu-Calvat, age fourteen, and Maximin Giraud, age eleven, were tending their father's cattle some miles from remote La Salette-Fallavaux, in the Alps. When they returned home that day, they reported seeing a beautiful woman who had appeared in a circle of bright light. She was seated, they said, and she was weeping. The woman stood and beckoned the youngsters to come closer. At first she spoke in French, but the two did not understand her, so she then spoke in their regional dialect.

The woman spoke to Melanie and Maximin about her son. She said that his arm was heavy, and she was tired of restraining it. She scolded the people, the children said, for working on Sundays and for using her son's name in curses. She also warned that there would be grim consequences if people did not repent in these matters. The woman instructed the two to say their prayers every day without fail, even if all they said was an Our Father and a Hail Mary. She told Melanie and Maximin to "make this known to all my people," and then, rising into the air, she disappeared.

This was the story the two young people told. They did not say that the woman they had seen was the Blessed Virgin Mary, although those who heard the story immediately identified her as such. As word began to spread, faith in the apparition expressed itself in various ways. People began to drink from a spring discovered at the place where the lady appeared, in the hope that the water would have healing powers. Melanie and Maximin pointed out the stone on which the lady had sat, and people broke off pieces, some people even grinding up bits of the stone to eat or drink with water from the spring. Cures were reported—miracles.

Melanie and Maximin were grilled repeatedly about their story, but they never changed even the slightest detail about what they had seen and heard. The local bishop, whose name was de Brouillard, began an intense investigation that lasted five years and sometimes caused considerable controversy. Finally, however, in November 1851, the bishop announced that he approved "the cult of Our Lady of La Salette," and he himself laid the cornerstone for a basilica to be built in her honor. Richard Beyer notes, "It is hard to imagine today the impact of the apparition. La Salette gave birth to a great movement of prayer, of conversion, and of commitment.... Christians everywhere saw or felt its influence,"[6] directly or through religious orders, the Missionaries of Our Lady of La Salette or the Sisters of La Salette.

Devotion to Our Lady of La Salette has cooled considerably, but images of her are easily recognizable. In these images, Mary wears a unique crucifix with a hammer suspended below one side of the crossbar and pincers below the other. The meaning of these symbols is uncertain.

Our Lady of Lourdes

The most popular Marian apparition site in the world is in Lourdes, France, in the northern foothills of the French Pyrénées. On February 11, 1858, an uneducated young girl named Bernarde-Marie (later popularized to Bernadette) Soubirous was collecting firewood with her sister and a friend. The three girls were dressed in virtual rags, scrounging for anything they could take home to burn for heat.

Bernadette, starving and sick, saw a "soft glow" in a hollowed out area of a high rock cliff called Massabielle. In the glow she saw a beautiful woman who gestured to Bernadette to come closer, though Bernadette was motionless with fear. Bernadette described what she saw: "a lady wearing a lovely white dress with a bright belt. On top of each of her feet was a pale yellow rose, the same color as her rosary beads."[7]

She testified that she wanted to make the sign of the cross; she could not do so, but the lady did make the sign. And as Bernadette prayed the Rosary, the lady moved the beads of her own rosary through her fingers. "When I stopped saying the Hail Mary," Bernadette wrote, "she immediately vanished."

The two other girls found their companion kneeling, motionless, staring up at the cave. When they looked, trying to see what Bernadette was looking at, they saw nothing unusual. They shook Bernadette out of her transfixed state, and she told them what she had seen—to their disbelief.

When the girls returned home and reported what had happened, Bernadette was punished and scolded and told not to go back to the site. All the same, Bernadette and the two other girls returned, this time with holy water from the parish church. When the beautiful woman appeared again, Bernadette tossed holy water at her, which made the woman smile.

At this point, Bernadette's friend climbed up above the cliff and pushed a large rock over the edge, which landed with a thud near Bernadette, who just continued gazing at her vision. Over the next few weeks, Bernadette saw the beautiful woman many times, without ever discovering her name. In her regional dialect, she simply referred to the woman as Aquero, meaning "that one." Bernadette said:

I went back each day for fifteen days, and each time, except one Monday and one Friday, the lady appeared and told me to look for a stream and wash in it and to see that the priests built a chapel there. I must also pray, she said, for the conversion of sinners. I asked her many times what she meant by that, but she only smiled. Finally, with outstretched arms and eyes looking up to heaven, she told me she was the Immaculate Conception.[8]

As news of Bernadette's visions spread, hundreds of people came to follow her to the grotto each day. On February 25 or 26, the woman told Bernadette to dig in the dirt just inside the cave. She obeyed, and the dirt grew muddy.... By the next day, the spring produced twenty-five thousand gallons of fresh, clear water and continued to do so daily. Within hours of the spring's appearance, a blind man who washed his eyes in the water was able to see again. A woman with a paralyzed hand plunged it into the water and regained its full use.

The phrase "Immaculate Conception" was not familiar to Bernadette. In fact, its meaning was explained to her over and over again in the days to come, but it was a long time, after she learned to read and write, before full comprehension sank in.

Six years later Bernadette joined a convent of the Sisters of Nevers, where she worked in the infirmary. She died of tuberculosis on April 16, 1879, at age thirty-five. She was canonized a saint in 1933, on December 8, the Feast of the Immaculate Conception. Miracles continue to this day at Lourdes—although most of them are not of a physical nature—and it is probably the most popular Marian pilgrimage site in the world.

Our Lady of Fátima

Between May and October of 1917, the Blessed Virgin Mary appeared six times to three Portuguese shepherd children, Lucia Santos and her cousins, Francisco and Jacinta Marto. When

What Authority Do Authenticated Apparitions Have?

Apparitions, visions, and other unusual occurrences attributed directly or indirectly to Mary may or may not be believed. None of them can ever be regarded as essential to Christian faith, whether they are approved by the official Church or not. If these phenomena do have any final authority, they are authoritative only for those who directly and immediately experience them. No one but the recipient(s) can be bound in conscience by whatever is communicated.

In any case, the "contents" (messages, directives, etc.) of such events can never be placed on a par with the Gospel itself, neither in terms of their authority nor in terms of the attention they elicit or demand. Those "contents," in turn, must always be measured against the totality of the Christian faith and must not contradict or contravene any essential component of that faith.

Richard P. McBrien[9]

these events were publicized, they captivated the attention of a world embroiled in the horrors of World War I. Mary gave the three children "secrets," some of which have not been revealed even today.

The Fátima apparitions began in the spring of 1916 when a young man appeared to the three children and identified himself as the angel of peace. He taught the children to pray and make sacrifices in a particular way, then departed. During the twelve months that followed, the three children followed the instructions they were given. Then in May 1917, while shepherding near the Cova da Iria, they saw a beautiful lady dressed in white surrounded by rays of brilliant light.

The woman told the children to not be afraid and to return on the thirteenth day of each month, until October, when she would reveal her identity and what she wanted them to do. The woman also told the children to pray the Rosary every day. When the children's immediate and extended family learned about the vision, they applied intense pressure, to make the children admit that they had concocted their story. But the children remained firmly insistent that they had told the truth.

Most adults couldn't believe that Mary would appear to mere children and tell them simply to pray the Rosary. But the woman promised the children that she would give a sign that would convince the skeptics. On the thirteenth day of each month, the children went back to the Cova da Iria. During these visits they received apocalyptic visions and dire predictions about the future. The woman announced that she wanted to have Russia dedicated to her Immaculate Heart. She also requested that people receive Holy Communion to make up for sins on the first Saturday of each month.

In the final appearance, October 13, 1917, the woman told the children that she was Our Lady of the Rosary and that she wanted a shrine built on the site of her apparitions. As she disappeared from the children's sight, the crowd (some seven hundred thousand) that had gathered saw what has come to be called the Miracle of the Sun. In the midst of a tremendous downpour, the rain suddenly stopped, and the sun came out. Witnesses later reported that they saw the sun "dance" in the sky then plunge toward the earth.

Many people, overcome by this, fell to their knees, crying out to God to save them. At this, the sun returned to its place, and the rain-drenched pilgrims were suddenly dry and comfortable. Meanwhile, the three children saw new visions of the Holy Family, Mary as the Sorrowful Mother with Jesus, and Mary as Our Lady of Mount Carmel.

The apparitions of Fátima were declared authentic by the bishop of Leiria on October 13, 1930. Interest in the Fátima story subsequently increased, particularly during and after World War II, with the rise of the Soviet Union. The famous "third secret" of Fátima has never been revealed to anyone but popes; such secrecy has generated rumors that continue to fuel sensationalist journalism. Wild, unfounded stories circulate about popes reading the "third secret" and fainting dead away. Equally fantastic stories say that the pope keeps the "third secret" locked in his private quarters or concealed on his own person at all times.

The truth is that the "third secret" has been passed along from one pope to another down to the present time, and each one decides whether or not to reveal the secret. So far, the secret remains a secret, and that is all anyone knows.

The traditional representation of Our Lady of Fátima—Our Lady of the Rosary—shows her in a simple gown and mantle of white bordered with blue, her hands folded in prayer and holding a white rosary. She is also always depicted wearing a jeweled crown. The Feast of Our Lady of the Rosary is October 7.

Unauthenticated Apparitions
During the twentieth century, reports of appearances by the Blessed Virgin Mary surfaced with regularity. People in Ireland, Belgium, Italy, Canada, and the United States announced that Mary had appeared to them, and in each case the church launched official investigations.

The recently claimed apparition that attracted the most attention was in Medjugorje, in Bosnia. In 1981 six children began to report appearances by Mary involving secrets, announcements about future events, and admonitions to prayer and penance. The site of the reported apparitions attracted people from the world over, and apparently they continue to the present day. "The Catholic church has withheld judgment of the Medjugorje events, until the official investigating commission reports its findings, probably not before the apparitions end."[10]

Conclusions

Marian apparitions have received considerable attention in the last forty years. The Marian shrine at Lourdes, France, and the shrine to Our Lady of Guadalupe, in Mexico City, continue to attract countless pilgrims every year. Purported apparitions of Mary at Medjugorje attracted thousands of pilgrims in the 1980s and early 1990s.

More than a few Catholics remain concerned about the apocalyptic and individualistic messages connected with Marian apparition sites, the most recent example being Medjugorje. Other Catholics conclude that apparitions are complex and prefer to reserve judgment.

While many people find apparitions of Mary helpful to their faith, many others do not. The Catholic Church always insists that even authenticated apparitions constitute private revelation and add nothing to what we already know of God in and through Christ. Therefore, belief in Marian apparitions is completely optional.

As one theologian explains:

No Catholic ... is required to believe even in private revelations associated with Marian apparitions that have been approved by the Church for devotional purposes, e.g., Lourdes and Fátima. At the same time, Catholics have every reason and right to be skeptical of alleged private revelations that have not been approved by the Church or, what is worse, have been specifically disapproved.[11]

As we turn to a discussion of Mary in modern times, keep in mind the influence of these apparitions, which have become known around the whole Christian world.

CHAPTER FIVE

Mary in Modern Catholic Thought

During the nineteenth and twentieth centuries, developments took place in the theology of Mary and in popular devotion to Mary that will affect Catholicism for the twenty-first century and beyond. Fortunately, the upshot of it all appears to be a healthier, more balanced understanding of, and devotion to, the Mother of Jesus. Yet the mystery of who she is and of her place in the life of faith is, if anything, more remarkable than ever.

Nineteenth Century

By the nineteenth century, devotion to Mary had become a hallmark of Catholicism. Yet, as Sally Cunneen explains, "Both Catholics and Protestants lacked balance in their approach to Mary, largely because of their mutual isolation."[1]

The intensity of Catholic enthusiasm for Marian apparitions during this time, particularly those at Lourdes, France, only increased Protestant belief that devotion to Mary was nonscriptural and bordered on idol worship. It is easy to sympathize with this Protestant distrust in the face of some of the popular Marian devotional writing of the time. The works of St. Lawrence of Brindisi (d. 1619), for example, were very popular during the nineteenth century. Lawrence declared that Mary was similar to Christ in "nature, grace, virtue, dignity, and glory." Describing the power of a man's passion for a beautiful woman, "she causes him to rave and causes the lover to go out of his mind," he says, "the Virgin could do this with God himself."[2]

An eighteenth-century romanticized devotional book, *The Glories of Mary*, by St. Alphonsus Liguori (d. 1787), founder of the Redemptorist order, was very popular and had wide influence on popular Catholic piety in the late nineteenth and early twentieth centuries. This book declared that "all graces that God gives to men pass through the hands of Mary." Liguori portrayed Mary as "the compassionate and wise spouse of an angry husband-God who, without her, might at any time do something he would later regret."[3]

In Europe and North America, it became the custom, for devotional purposes, to wear the "Miraculous Medal," a small oval-shaped picture of Mary worn on a necklace chain, inspired by the 1830 visions of Catherine Labouré in France. The medal honors the Immaculate Conception.

On December 8, 1854, Pope Pius IX declared the Immaculate Conception of Mary to be Catholic dogma. Dogma means "a definitive, or infallible, teaching of the Church."[4] Again, there is no direct support for this teaching in Scripture, although the official document signed by Pius IX refers to certain scriptural texts "that by extension can support it."[5] These references include Genesis 3:15 (pledge of victory over the serpent); Luke 1:28 (the angel greets Mary as "favored one"); and Luke 1:42 (Elizabeth's praise for Mary: "Blessed are you among women").

Toward the end of the nineteenth century, a level-headed perspective on Mary came from Cardinal John Henry Newman, the great English convert to Catholicism from Anglicanism. Newman, whose life spanned almost the entire nineteenth century, thought of Mary not in sentimental ways but first of all as a human disciple of Christ. For Newman, Mary should be our guide as we reflect on God's presence within. He said that Mary is the model of faith in the face of doubt. He wanted not only typical believers but also intellectuals to be comfortable with Mary. Anticipating Vatican II by nearly a century, and following the lead of fourth- and fifth-century theologians such as St. Augustine and St. Ambrose, Newman saw Mary as a symbol of the church. He also held up Mary as an example of how Christians should pray:

> She is the great exemplar of prayer in a generation which emphatically denies the power of prayer in toto, which determines that fatal laws govern the universe, that there cannot be any direct communication between earth and heaven, that God cannot visit his own earth, and that man cannot influence his own providence.[6]

John Henry Newman took Mary's humanity seriously at a time when she was raised by many pious writers almost to the same level as Christ himself. He saw Mary as our companion on our pilgrimage through life and as a model of faith for all believers, ideas that would be embraced, ratified, and made normative for the whole church by Vatican II in the mid-1960s.

Twentieth Century

Popular devotion to Mary during the early 1900s centered on the Immaculate Conception, the Immaculate Heart (see discussion of this feast day in chapter 6), and—especially in the late 1940s and 1950s—May devotions. May is considered Mary's special month. In Catholic schools, on the first of May, girls processed, sang Marian hymns, and placed a crown of flowers on the head of a statue of Mary. Girls considered it a high honor when chosen to place the crown of flowers on the statue of the Blessed Virgin.

Marian devotions flourished during the 1940s and 1950s. Catholic girls and young women were taught to cultivate a "Marylike" modesty in how they dressed and behaved. As the Catholic church moved toward Vatican II, in the mid-1960s, devotion to Mary was at one of its highest points in history. Pilgrimages to Fátima and Lourdes were popular.

Father Patrick Peyton's Rosary Crusades held huge gatherings across the country in sports stadiums and auditoriums at which the Rosary prayer was repeated en masse. Father Peyton gave stirring speeches on devotion to Mary, local bishops basked on stage in Father Peyton's aura, and whole families went home promising to pray the Rosary together daily. Father Peyton's slogan became a rallying cry: "The family that prays together stays together."

After the War, people flocked to the sites of Marian apparitions, such as Lourdes and Fátima, among others. Papal pronouncements (encyclicals) on Mary increased interest in her. Marian years (whole years dedicated by the pope to Mary), Marian congresses, and new feasts of Mary, such as the Queenship of Mary, established in 1954, all contributed to keeping Mary prominent in Catholic life.

In the early twentieth century, there was considerable debate about whether it would be appropriate to give Mary the titles Co-redemptrix and Mediatrix of All Graces. Neither title has ever received official church approval. The former idea seemed to reduce Jesus to but half of a team of redeemers. The latter depends on the former and seems to imply that there is the possibility of a relationship with Christ only by going through Mary first. Vatican II insisted that Mary's role in the salvation of humankind is completely subordinate to that of Christ, "the one Mediator" for everyone.[7]

In 1950 belief in the Assumption of Mary was pronounced official Catholic dogma. Modern theological reflection on the dogma of the Assumption centers on the ultimate "victory of God's grace, freely given in Christ, which consecrates and ultimately saves the whole person, both body and soul...." The Assumption of Mary, in other words, is a symbol of "the final destiny of all the redeemed in Christ." This dogma "signifies to all persons ... that the loving power of God will prevail."[8]

As when the Immaculate Conception was made dogma, Protestants protested vigorously, though there was almost universal Catholic support for both teachings. Both of these dogmas are stumbling blocks when it comes to ecumenical discussions. Protestants do not like it that both teachings are set forth as binding on conscience when neither has direct scriptural evidence. Catholic-Protestant dialogues continue to discuss this problem, and various solutions have been offered, though none have been officially accepted by either side.

For Catholics, the dogmas of the Immaculate Conception and Assumption of Mary reflect, first, God's unlimited saving power to liberate and heal us in this world and the next. Obviously, of course, they also remind us of Mary's utterly unique status and her great and freely given love for God.

As the church faced the Second Vatican Council (1962–65), which had the daunting task of trying to move the entire church into the late twentieth century, theologians and other influential Catholics were of two minds when it came to Mary. Some Catholics wanted the Council to declare another Marian dogma, perhaps establishing infallibly Mary as Co-redemptrix and Mediatrix of All Graces. Others wanted to bring Marian devotion more into line with Scripture, the liturgy, and the traditions of the early church.

Rather than issue a separate document on Mary, Vatican II decided, in what turned out to be the closest vote of the council, to include its teaching on Mary in its document *Lumen Gentium*, the Dogmatic Constitution on the Church. This choice brought to a close the isolation of the theology of Mary from the rest of Catholic theology and situated it in the main body of Catholic thought. Chapter 8 of *Lumen Gentium* is titled "The Role of the Blessed Virgin Mary, Mother of God, in the Mystery of Christ and the Church."

Chapter 8 of *Lumen Gentium*, the key chapter on Mary, presents her as essentially a woman of faith who heard and responded without reservation to God's Word in her life, and by doing this she "gave Life to the world."[9] Therefore she is "acknowledged and honored as being truly the Mother of God and of the redeemer."

Redeemed, in a more exalted fashion, by reason of the merits of her Son and united to him by a close and indissoluble tie, she is endowed with the high office and dignity of the Mother of the Son of God, and therefore she is also the beloved daughter of the Father and the temple of the Holy Spirit.

Therefore Mary "far surpasses all creatures, both in heaven and on earth," and she is "united to all those who are saved...." Mary is the outstanding model of faith and charity, so the church, meaning all of us, "honors her with filial affection and devotion as a most beloved mother." The important thing to notice here is that Vatican II clearly relates Mary's unique status to her connection with Jesus and her wholehearted response to God's Word in faith.

At the same time, *Lumen Gentium* insists that Mary is a fully human being who is just as much in need of redemption as any other human being. Her Immaculate Conception does not set her apart from the need that all human beings have for salvation in Christ. "[B]eing of the race of Adam, she is … united to all those who are to be saved." Mary is the ultimate model for our pilgrimage of faith.

Mary is the faithful disciple of Christ whose pilgrimage has come to a joyful conclusion. She above all other saints is the one who offers hope to those still on pilgrimage.

This *Lumen Gentium* chapter views Mary in the context of the communion of saints, although she is understood to be a "pre-eminent and … wholly unique member of the Church.…"

Vatican II reemphasizes the humanity and faith of Mary, insisting that she both "occupies a place in the Church which is highest after Christ and also closest to us." Mary lived her life as a journey of faith. She is the member of the church who serves as a model of faith, love, and union with Christ. The council insists that to call upon Mary as "Advocate, Helper, Benefactress, and Mediatrix" neither takes anything away from nor adds anything to the role of Christ as sole Mediator of grace. Rather:

No creature could ever be counted along with the Incarnate Word and Redeemer; but just as the priesthood of Christ is shared in various ways both by his ministers and the faithful, and as the one goodness of God is radiated in different ways among his creatures, so also the unique mediation of the Redeemer does not exclude but rather gives rise to a manifold cooperation which is but a sharing in this one source.

In other words, Mary simply does what every member of the communion of saints does, although she does it in a unique manner given her special status as the *Theotokos* (God-bearer, Mother of God). Just as we pray for one another, and we can petition the saints in heaven to pray for us, so we can ask her to pray for us, as well, and her prayers are effective because she exercises a special "ministry," as it were, that is an exercise of the

Merton's Mary

One of the most popular and influential American Catholics of the twentieth century was Thomas Merton (1915–68), a Trappist monk who was a writer, poet, and social commentator. In his book *New Seeds of Contemplation*, Merton wrote of Mary:

The genuine significance of Catholic devotion to Mary is to be seen in the light of the Incarnation itself. The Church cannot separate the Son and the Mother. Because the Church conceives of the Incarnation as God's descent into flesh and into time, and His great gift of Himself to His creatures, she also believes that the one who was closest to Him in this great mystery was the one who participated most perfectly in the gift. When a room is heated by an open fire, surely there is nothing strange in the fact that those who stand closest to the fireplace are the ones who are warmest. And when God comes into the world through the instrumentality of one of His servants, then there is nothing surprising about the fact that His chosen instrument should have the greatest and most intimate share in the divine gift.[10]

one mediation of God's grace by Christ. "The Church does not hesitate to profess this subordinate role of Mary," the council declares, "… so that encouraged by this maternal help they may the more closely adhere" to Christ.

Vatican II also teaches that Mary is, in fact, "a type of the Church in the order of faith, charity, and perfect union with Christ." Mary is what the church strives to be, dedicated in discipleship and mother to all the faithful.

This important chapter in one of the central documents of Vatican II concludes by explaining that the devotion given to Mary is different, in essence, from the worship we give to God alone. The council advises believers neither to exaggerate nor to minimize the importance of devotion to Mary. In truth, it sometimes seems that Catholics find it difficult to maintain this balance. Either we are virtually indifferent toward Mary or we make too much of her. A healthy Christian faith includes a warm devotion to Mary, but its central focus is always on Christ.

When the Second Vatican Council turned its attention to Mary and her place in Catholicism, the work of one theologian, Father Karl Rahner, S.J., was particularly influential. Rahner suggested, for example, that the Immaculate Conception be thought of as reflecting the fact that from the moment of her conception in her mother's womb Mary benefited from the saving action of Christ, even before it happened in the historical sense. The Assumption reflects the same fact at the end of Mary's life, Rahner said. The whole person of Mary, body and soul, is united with God, which is what all of us ultimately hope for, as well.

For Rahner, the dogmas of the Immaculate Conception and Assumption give us the faith and hope that *our* lives are graced from conception to death, too. They give us the hope that ultimately grace will be victorious in our lives, and we, like Mary, will find ourselves cradled in God's love following natural death. In other words, Mary's story offers us a model and a hope for all human life, "from the cradle to the grave." In Rahner's own words:

> The ideal picture we have before us must naturally be determined by Christ. For this reason, it cannot be he, so it must be realized by some other person through a perfect following of him. Now the ideal of perfect openness to Christ is found concretely realized in Mary. She is the one who is perfectly redeemed. And, of course, she is perfectly redeemed in a very definite way belonging to her alone! But this way is at the same time the ideal case, the perfect fulfillment of what is and must be the law and goal of our lives through the inner structure of our existence in grace.[11]

Of course, Vatican II had a significant concern for the impact of Catholic attitudes toward Mary on relations with other churches. The council declared that Catholicism does not think of Mary as a supernatural go-between to rescue us from an angry Christ. Rather, Mary, along with all the other saints, participates in the mediation of Christ. Vatican II does not speak of Mary as "the number-one saint," but this idea is perfectly compatible with the Vatican II teachings on Mary. When we ask Mary and the other saints to pray for us, this is simply a witness to our conviction that the concern of the church's members for one another continues beyond natural death. Just as we pray for one another here on earth, so those who have passed into eternity may continue to pray for those still on their earthly pilgrimage.

This does not take away from the truth that Christ is the one and only Mediator between God and human beings. "[T]he unique mediation of the Redeemer does not exclude but rather gives rise to a manifold cooperation which is but a sharing in this one source."[12]

Vatican II gave inspiration and guidance for a renewed devotion to Mary as the model for Christian faith in response to God's invitation. Instead of a renewed interest in Marian devotion, however, the decades following Vatican II saw a dramatic decrease of interest in her, especially in the so-called developed nations of North America and Western Europe. Almost no theologians turned their attention to thinking about Mary and her place in the Christian life. Oddly enough, even though Vatican II gave her a major place in its Dogmatic Constitution on the Church, Mary did not play a significant role in post-Vatican II theological reflection on the nature and purpose of the church. On the level of popular piety, among those who retained a lively devotion to Mary, the teachings of Vatican II had little impact.

One possible reason for the dramatic drop-off in Marian devotion may have come from Vatican II, also. Theologian Mary E. Hines suggests:

The conciliar document on ecumenism postulates the theory of a hierarchy of truths of Christian belief....Within this hierarchy, truths concerning the self-revealing God, Jesus Christ, the Church, and a renewed anthropology commanded the most attention in the immediate postconciliar period. Mary, while important, was considered to belong to a secondary level of truths of faith and thus took a back seat to more central concerns of liturgical and ecclesial renewal.[13]

It also seems that chapter 8 of *Lumen Gentium* primarily limited itself to addressing past imbalances in Marian devotion. While it emphasized the connection between Mary and the church, it did not provide any clear direction for the future and a revitalized teaching of Mary. In *Lumen Gentium* we find no attempt to relate Mary to the modern world, which is otherwise such a powerful characteristic of the Vatican II documents. The council warned against getting carried away with devotion to Mary, but it provided no guidelines for a healthy, balanced Marian devotion.

Since Vatican II, a 1974 apostolic exhortation of Pope Paul VI, *Marialis Cultus,* provided a most constructive and helpful contribution to a renewed Mariology. This is particularly true with regard to standards for popular devotion to Mary. *Marialis Cultus* tries to revitalize popular Marian devotion within the spirit of Vatican II. In this document Pope Paul VI says that "certain practices of piety that not long ago seemed suitable for expressing the religious sentiment of individuals and religious communities seem today inadequate because they are linked with social and cultural patterns of the past."[14]

Among contemporary realities that a renewed theology of Mary must take into account, Pope Paul VI wrote, is the changed status of women in society. Women who take for granted that they have rights equal to those of men will not be inspired if Mary is presented to them as a passive figure submissive to men in all things. This is, virtually, a feminist view of Mary not explicitly mentioned in the earlier history of Catholic devotion to Mary.

Since the late 1980s, there has been a renewed interest in Mariology, the theology of Mary. In particular, the so-called liberation theology movement of the Third World and feminist theology have shown remarkable interest in Mary. In both cases, oppressed populations find in Mary a source of inspiration. Liberation theology finds in Mary's Magnificat (Luke 1:46-55) considerable encouragement for efforts to aid poor and oppressed peoples. The Mary of the Magnificat is seen as one who knows, firsthand, the meaning of God's plan for the liberation for the poor of the earth. A document issued by the Third General Conference of the Latin American Episcopate, in 1979, says:

> The Magnificat mirrors the soul of Mary. In that canticle we find the culmination of the spirituality of Yahweh's poor and lowly, and of the prophetic strain in the Old Testament.... In the Magnificat she presents herself as the model for all ... those who do not passively accept the adverse circumstances of personal and social life and who are not victims of "alienation" ... but who instead join with her in proclaiming that God is the "avenger of the lowly" and will, if need be, "depose the mighty from their thrones."[15]

In other words, this document presents Mary as actively involved in the ministry of Jesus. She does not sit passively by, merely acquiescing to God's will, but willingly, actively participates in the mission of her son.

Latin American theologian Leonardo Boff, in his 1987 book *The Maternal Face of God*, wrote: "It is our task ... to develop a prophetic image of Mary as a strong, determined woman, the woman committed to the messianic liberation of the poor from the historical social injustices under which they suffer."[16]

As noteworthy as liberation theology's interest in Mary certainly is, it seems to have had little, if any, impact on popular

Marian devotion. The image of Our Lady of Guadalupe, however, gives evidence of blending effectively popular Marian devotion and the Mary of the Magnificat embraced by liberation theology. In Latin America and Central America, theologians, clergy, and ordinary believers find in Our Lady of Guadalupe an image they can relate to in a lively fashion.

Beginning in the 1970s, feminist theology turned its attention, albeit cautiously, to Mary, to see if she could serve as a source of liberation for women within Catholicism. Turning away from an interpretation of Mary that they saw as reinforcing women's secondary status in both society and the church, feminist theologians asked if perhaps Mary herself was part of the problem. Was it not true, these theologians asked, that Mary had become little more than "a product of male projections about the 'ideal woman,' the 'eternal feminine'"?[17]

Aware of this negative theological view, other feminist theologians discussed a more positive approach to Mary. Vatican II offered the perspective on Mary as a model of the church, and Pope Paul VI contributed the image of Mary as the ideal disciple who heard the Word of God and acted on it. The new feminist perspective began with these images then turned to the work of contemporary Scripture scholarship, in particular a collaborative book authored by the Lutheran-Roman Catholic Dialogue, *Mary in the New Testament.*[18]

This study highlighted how little we actually know about the historical Mary. The few times she appears in the New Testament are clearly for theological purposes, and accounts differ as to what she did and when and why. In the Gospel of Luke, for example, Mary is the central character, but in Matthew's Gospel her role seems subservient to that of Joseph. Mary's historical fuzziness allows modern thinkers and artists to reflect on her in a creative manner while remaining faithful to the information we do get about her from the New Testament.

Drawing on the Gospels of Luke and Matthew, contemporary writers are free to suggest that we think of Mary by titles such as Mother of the Homeless, Widowed Mother, Mother of a Political Prisoner, Unwed Mother, Liberator of the Oppressed, Seeker of Sanctuary, and First Disciple.[19]

Finally, it is noteworthy that in *The Mary Myth*—a remarkably creative contribution to the "reinvention" of Mary for our time—Father Andrew M. Greeley wrote what could, but so far has not, become a foundational text for a renewed Mariology to enrich the lives of Christians of many classes, cultures, and traditions. For Greeley, Mary reveals something about God that we are unlikely to find anyplace else. Mary reveals God's smiling, maternal love.[20]

Much remains to be done to reincorporate Marian devotion into Catholic life, yet there is no more worthy project.[21] For "it remains the case that remembering her, thanking God for her, drawing on her example, and asking for her prayers is an abiding and deeply rooted characteristic of the Catholic community."[22]

CHAPTER SIX

Mary in the Liturgical Life of the Church

D evotion to Mary is well represented in the church's liturgy and liturgical calendar. Today in the post-Vatican II period, devotion to Mary in the liturgy is clearly centered on Christ. A morning hymn from the Liturgy of the Hours illustrates this Christ-centered focus. For fourteen lines it compares Mary and Jesus, Jesus always being the fuller or the richer part. For example:

> Mary the root, Christ the Mystic Vine;
> Mary the grape, Christ the Sacred Wine!

Mary and the Mass
Whenever the Eucharist or Mass is celebrated, the prayers always include a remembrance of Mary, in the company of the apostles, martyrs, and all the saints. In Eucharistic Prayer I, for example, we pray: "In union with the whole Church we honor Mary, the ever-virgin Mother of Jesus Christ our Lord and God."

The *Catechism of the Catholic Church* goes so far as to say, quoting Pope Paul VI's *Marialis Cultus,* that devotion to Mary is "intrinsic to Christian worship." The Catechism adds, however, that devotion to Mary in the liturgy is both essentially different from the worship of God and "fosters" this worship.[1]

Mary and the Liturgical Calendar

At various times during the liturgical year, which begins with Advent, we—the church—honor Mary through various liturgical observances.

In descending liturgical importance, these include four solemnities or solemn feasts, three feasts, and five memorials, and various optional memorials.

Mary and the Season of Advent

The liturgical church year begins with Advent, the four weeks prior to Christmas. There are many liturgical references to Mary during this season of hope and expectation. Most of these occur between December 17 and 24, in particular on the Sunday just prior to Christmas, when we hear the Old Testament prophecies about the virgin Mother and the Messiah. The Gospel readings during these eight days speak of the birth of Christ and his forerunner, John the Baptist, the child born to Mary's older relative, Elizabeth.

Solemnity of the Immaculate Conception

The main Marian liturgical event during Advent is the Solemnity of the Immaculate Conception on December 8.

Again, the Immaculate Conception refers to Mary's own conception; though she had a natural conception—a human mother and father—her human nature was never affected by original sin. (See chapters 3 and 5.)

In the Western church, a December 8 celebration of the Immaculate Conception is noted, with some controversy, in France in the twelfth century, having earlier roots in England and, before that, the Eastern church.[2]

The celebration of the Immaculate Conception is right at

home during Advent; Mary is the ultimate example and model of what it means to be ready, hopeful, and filled with faith while looking forward to the coming of Christ. Mary is the archetype of the people of God, the church, getting ready to celebrate its beginning at the birth of Christ.

This poem by Maurice Francis Egan is appropriate for this feast day.

> O moon, O symbol of our Lady's whiteness;
> O snow, O symbol of our Lady's heart
> O night, chaste night, bejewelled with argent brightness,
> How sweet, how bright, how loving, kind thou art!
> O miracle; tomorrow and tomorrow,
> In tender reverence, shall no praise abate
> For from all seasons shall we new jewels borrow
> To deck the Mother born Immaculate.[3]

Our Lady of Guadalupe

The Memorial of Our Lady of Guadalupe, December 12, is celebrated only in the Americas and has more cultural significance throughout Latin America and among Hispanic populations in North America than most of the Marian solemn feast days celebrating scriptural events. This memorial celebrates the appearance of Mary in 1531 to an Aztec Indian peasant, Juan Diego. (For the complete story, see chapter 4.)

Mary and the Christmas Season

The Christmas season lasts about two weeks, from Christmas Day until Epiphany, which the Roman Catholic church celebrates on the second Sunday after Christmas (not on January 6, as does the Anglican community). Throughout these two weeks, the liturgy calls us to honor Mary as we worship Christ.

Christmas Day

Though Christmas Day is a feast of Christ, not of Mary, it's virtually impossible to read about, think about, sing about, or celebrate the birth of the Christ child without immediate reference to his mother, Mary. The Christmas liturgy celebrates the birth of Christ in the context of his place in his human family of Mary and Joseph.

One stanza of a fourth-century Christmas carol by Aurelius Clemens Prudentius concisely summarizes Mary's place in the Christmas story:

O that ever-blessed birthday,
When the Virgin, full of grace,
By the Holy Ghost conceiving,
Bare the Savior of our race;
And that Child, the world's Redeemer,
First displayed his sacred face,
Evermore and evermore!

The Holy Family

The Sunday following Christmas is the Feast of the Holy Family. Although not a specifically Marian liturgical event, it is an appropriate time to recall Jesus' family and the importance of his relationships with his human parents, Mary and Joseph. In recent decades, many parishes also use Holy Family Sunday to focus on the family, in its various forms, as the church's most basic unit.[4] Pope John Paul II expressed the meaning of this teaching concisely: "The family in fact is the basic unit of society and of the Church. It is 'the domestic church.' Families are those living cells which come together to form the very substance of parish life."[5]

The Solemnity of Mary the Mother of God

The first day of January is the Solemnity of Mary the Mother of God, the most important Marian observance during the liturgical year. On this day we recall the vitally important part played by Mary in the foundational events of Christian history and in the mystery of salvation. Upon her "yes" depended the coming into human history of Jesus the Christ, the Son of God. Because she had human freedom, she had a choice, and she chose to cooperate with God in accomplishing his will for the salvation of humankind. The Solemnity of Mary the Mother of God celebrates the Christ-centered focus of her life and faith and calls us to the same focus, following her example.

Epiphany

The Feast of the Epiphany is of ancient origin, going back to at least the fourth century. On the Feast of the Epiphany, we recall the visit of the Magi to see the Christ child and his mother. While, again, this is not a specifically Marian liturgical celebration, Mary figures prominently in its observance. The gentile Magi remind us that Christ came into the world for all peoples, and it is Mary who holds the infant Messiah and presents him to the Magi. It is Mary who welcomes the wise men into the stable and presents Jesus to them, a reminder that Mary invites all people to accept faith in Christ.

The Presentation of the Lord

The Feast of the Presentation of the Lord, February 2, commemorates the event described in Luke 2:22-40, where Mary and Joseph bring the infant Jesus to the temple. In Eastern Orthodox traditions, this feast is known as the Purification, a reference to the ritual purification Mary, as a Jewish woman, was required to undergo following childbirth. In the Orthodox traditions, this feast sometimes includes processions of young girls dressed in festive white.

Our Lady of Lourdes

February 11 is the optional memorial of Our Lady of Lourdes. This day is a memorial of the most popular Marian apparition in modern times. (For more information, see chapter 4.)

The Solemnity of the Annunciation

The Annunciation of Our Lord is celebrated on March 25. This observance is also scriptural in origin, commemorating the "annunciation," or announcement, by the angel Gabriel to Mary that she would become the mother of Christ (see Luke 1:26-38). The Annunciation was first celebrated in the fifth century, during Advent. It was later moved to March 25, exactly nine months prior to the celebration of Christmas, but also at the vernal equinox, the beginning of spring.[6]

The thirteenth-century mystic St. Catherine the Great (d. 1301) had this vision:

On the Feast of the Annunciation I saw the heart of the Virgin Mother so bathed by the rivers of grace flowing out of the blessed Trinity that I understood the privilege Mary has of being the most powerful after God the Father, the most wise after God the Son, and the most kindly after God the Holy Spirit.[7]

The Visitation

May 31 marks the Feast of the Visitation, which recalls the visit of Mary to her older relative Elizabeth (see Luke 1:36-56). The

Our Mother of Perpetual Help

One of the most prominent nonliturgical devotions to Mary is to Our Mother of Perpetual Help. This devotion began, according to legend, when the Christ child was terrified by a vision of two angels who showed him the instruments that would be used in his suffering and death. Jesus ran to his mother and in his haste almost lost one of his sandals. The traditional icon picture of Our Mother of Perpetual Help shows Mary holding the child Jesus, one sandal dangling from his foot. Held safely in his mother's arms, Jesus' hands are held palms down in his mother's hands, a sign that the graces of salvation are in her care. Legend has it that this picture was painted by St. Luke, but the origins and age of the picture are unknown.

first words of Elizabeth's greeting to Mary are the second sentence in the prayer known as the Hail Mary: "Blessed are you among women, and blessed is the fruit of your womb...." This Luke passage, read on this day, includes one of the best known and most beloved canticles (poetic songs) in the New Testament, the Magnificat (from the first word, *magnifies*, in its Latin translation): "My soul magnifies the Lord, and my spirit rejoices in God my Savior."

The Immaculate Heart of Mary
This optional memorial does not fall on a specific date but on the Saturday after the second Sunday after Pentecost. This day recalls a Marian devotion to the Immaculate Heart of Mary that

originated in the seventeenth century by St. John Eudes (d. 1680), a French priest; with St. Margaret Mary Alacoque (d. 1690), he also originated the devotion to the Sacred Heart of Jesus, a devotion centered on the compassionate love of Christ.

The devotion to the Immaculate Heart of Mary was especially popular during the early 1800s and the 1940s and early 1950s. In 1942 Pope Pius XII consecrated the world to the Immaculate Heart of Mary. The symbol of Mary's Immaculate Heart refers to the doctrine of her Immaculate Conception and her compassionate love. Sometimes images of Mary as the Immaculate Heart show her heart pierced by a small sword, a symbol that refers to the event in the temple (see Luke 2:34-35) where Simeon says to Mary: "A sword will pierce your own soul too."

On this feast day in May 1982 Pope John Paul II prayed the following prayer "To the Immaculate Heart":

O Immaculate Heart! Help us to conquer the menace of evil, which so easily takes root in the hearts of the people of today, and whose immeasurable effects already weigh down upon our modern world and seem to block the paths towards the future!

From famine and war, deliver us.

From nuclear war, from incalculable self-destruction, from every kind of war, deliver us.

From sins against the life of man from its very beginning, deliver us....

Accept, O Mother of Christ, this cry laden with the sufferings of all individual human beings, laden with the suffering of whole societies.

Let there be revealed once more, in the history of the

world, your infinite power of merciful love. May it put a stop to evil. May it transform consciences. May your Immaculate Heart reveal for all the light of Hope.[8]

Our Lady of Mount Carmel

The optional memorial of Our Lady of Mount Carmel, July 16, is an example of a Marian devotion that began with a particular religious order, the Carmelites, and later became popular with the church as a whole. Our Lady of Mount Carmel is the title given to Mary as the patron of the Carmelite order.

According to legend, the Carmelite St. Simon Stock (d. 1265) asked Mary to give a special privilege to his order. So on a certain day, the Blessed Virgin appeared to him holding a brown scapular. (This is a long, shoulder-width piece of fabric with an opening for the head. As a garment the scapular covers one something like an apron that covers both front and back.) Giving the scapular, Mary said, "Here is the privilege I grant to you and to all children of Carmel. Whoever dies clothed in this habit shall be saved."[9]

It may be difficult to find meaning in devotion to Our Lady of Mount Carmel today. Still, Mary's expression of compassionate love for one particular religious order may be taken as an expression of her love for all in their particular needs.

Dedication of the Basilica of Saint Mary Major

August 5, the optional memorial of the Dedication of St. Mary Major, recalls the dedication of the first church in Rome named for the mother of Jesus: *Santa Maria Maggiore,* Great St. Mary's. St. Mary Major is located on Rome's Esquiline Hill. Constructed in the fourth century, the church was first called the Liberian Basilica, for the current pope, Liberius. It was restored and rededicated to the Virgin Mary by Pope Sixtus III, in about the year 435.

Liturgical books call this basilica St. Mary of the Snows. This name comes from a popular tradition in which Mary chose this place for a church dedicated to her by causing a miraculous summer snowfall on the site. According to the tradition, Mary appeared to a rich man named John who founded and endowed the church when Liberius was pope. This is probably merely a charming legend, because there is no historical record of the miracle of the snowfall until one hundred years after it was supposed to have happened.

To add to the legendary aura of the basilica, it is also sometimes called St. Mary *ad Praesepe* because it houses an alleged relic of the crib or manger in which Mary placed Jesus. Another charming legend, no doubt. Still, that a church would be named for Mary as early as 435 attests to the power of Marian devotion in the early church.

The Solemnity of the Assumption

On August 15 the church celebrates the doctrine that teaches that upon her death Mary was taken directly into heaven, body and soul. This dogma was officially announced by Pope Pius XII on November 1, 1950. Ninety-eight percent of the world's bishops agreed at the time that the tradition behind this teaching was sufficient.

There is no scriptural evidence for this infallible teaching, although traditionally the "woman clothed with the sun" described in Revelation 12 is cited. The early fathers of the church also said nothing about this. The first historical evidence for belief in Mary's assumption appears in the sixth century when her feast day blended in the popular imagination with an apocryphal account of her death, funeral, empty tomb, and bodily entrance into heaven. First in various Eastern churches, then by the seventh century in Rome as well, the main Marian feast day became a commemoration of Mary's bodily assumption into heaven.

Clearly the central meaning of the Assumption is to reaffirm that, however mysteriously, in some form the body participates in our ultimate eternal destiny. We will never become "ghosts" or "disembodied spirits." To be human is to be "embodied," just as Christ was following his resurrection, and as Mary was following her death and assumption.

The Queenship of Mary

The Memorial of the Queenship of Mary is August 22. This reflects the belief that following her assumption Mary became, metaphorically speaking, Queen of Heaven. In 1954 Pope Pius XII established the feast of Mary the Queen, to be celebrated on May 31. The current liturgical calendar, however, locates the observance one week after the Assumption.

This is a liturgical observance dominated by metaphor, a figure of speech that communicates truth as long as we do not take it literally. Crowns are made of precious metals and stones, and queens are earthly rulers in countries that have a monarchical governmental structure. To say that Mary was "crowned" as "queen" of heaven is to make a devotional point about Mary's special place in eternity. This belief is not an infallible dogma. To celebrate the queenship of Mary is simply to acknowledge her special role in the history of salvation and her unique status in eternity.

The Birth of Mary

The church celebrates the Feast of the Birth of Mary on September 8. We have no historical information about Mary's birth, of course, but some tradition is based on the apocryphal Infancy Gospel of James, discussed in chapter 2.

King Alfonsus the Wise of Castile is credited with a tribute to the birth of Mary that begins and ends with this stanza:

> Blessed was the day ...
> whereon God's Virgin Mother
> was brought forth.[10]

Our Lady of Sorrows

September 15 marks the Memorial of Our Lady of Sorrows. The feast was originally observed as a local feast in Germany in the fifteenth century on Good Friday, clearly aligning Mary's sorrow with Jesus' crucifixion. In the eighteenth century, Pope Benedict XIII made the feast universal to the whole church. In the nineteenth century, it was moved to September.[11]

Historically the image of Mary as sorrowing mother has engendered strong sympathy and devotion. In her popular life of Mary, Marie of Agreda (d. 1665) imagined that Mary

> prayed that she might be permitted to feel and participate in her virginal body all the pains of the wounds and tortures about to be undergone by Jesus. This petition was granted by the blessed Trinity, and the mother in consequence suffered all the torments of her most holy son in exact duplication.[12]

Primarily a devotional observance, on this day the call is to focus on Mary's compassion for her crucified son and thus grow in compassion ourselves for the suffering of other people.

Our Lady of the Rosary

October 7 is the Memorial of Our Lady of the Rosary. Another devotional observance, the purpose of this is to encourage the Rosary as a devotional prayer. (We will discuss the Rosary more fully in chapter 7.)

The Presentation of Mary

The final Marian liturgical observance of the year is the Memorial of the Presentation of Mary, November 21. Another observance that has apocryphal origins—again, in the Infancy Gospel of James—the purpose of this day is simply to encourage devotion to Mary.

Mary in the Liturgy of the Hours

Apart from the Eucharist, Mary is mentioned every day in the Liturgy of the Hours and prominently on those days when the Eucharist has a Marian theme. The Liturgy of the Hours is a regular schedule of psalms, scriptural and nonscriptural readings, and prayers used mainly by priests and members of religious orders and congregations, although some laity keep the schedule, too.

Every day's Vespers or Evening Prayer includes a reading or recitation of Mary's canticle of praise, the Magnificat (see Luke 1:46-55). There are many Marian hymns, and the prayers of intercession at the end of Morning and Evening Prayer frequently appeal to Mary for her prayers on our behalf. The Office of Readings often presents nonscriptural selections that encourage meditation on Mary and her faith. Excerpts from the writings of various saints and modern authors include poems, theology, and devotional works.

Mary in Other Rituals

Mary is mentioned prominently in other liturgical rituals as well. These include the baptismal rite, the Sacrament of Reconciliation (Confession), and the other sacraments. In all cases, however, Mary is mentioned as she is in the Eucharist, as the "lead saint," we might say, in invocations of the entire communion of saints. The idea, in all of these situations, is for Mary to help Christians develop a closer relationship with Christ. Sometimes at Catholic weddings, the bride will recite a special prayer to Mary or sing a traditional hymn to Mary.

CHAPTER SEVEN

Marian Devotions

C atholics also honor Mary by various nonliturgical devotional practices. These include the Rosary, pilgrimages to
various Marian sites such as Lourdes and Fátima, and the veneration of Marian icons, pictures, and statues.

Catholic spirituality welcomes the affective and emotional
side of human nature. We are whole people, including our feelings, therefore a balanced, mature spirituality includes a devotional component that takes advantage of specific "devotions"
and devotional prayers. "Devotional" here refers to the affective
component of a spirituality, where our feelings and emotions are
consciously included. "Devotions" refers to the prayer-forms we
use to nourish the "devotional" part of our spirituality. Thus we
nourish our "devotion to Mary" by using Marian "devotional"
prayers such as the Rosary.

A mature complete Catholic spirituality gravitates toward
balance. Even the Jesuits (Society of Jesus), known for their
emphasis on the intellectual life, meditate and pray using the
highly devotional and imaginative Spiritual Exercises of St.
Ignatius Loyola; these exercises encourage placing oneself in
Gospel scenes.

Therese Johnson Borchard defines "devotions" as "an
organized form of prayer, separate but related to the liturgy, that
deepens my personal relationship with God, strengthens my
commitment to the Christian community, and leads me to a
deeper understanding of the Paschal Mystery [the death and
resurrection of Christ], the reality to which my faith continually
looks."[1]

Marian devotions, in particular, help us to live out a deeper faith and a greater dedication to the gospel. In the words of Vatican II:

Let the faithful remember ... that true devotion consists neither in sterile nor transitory affection, nor in a certain vain credulity, but proceeds from true faith, by which we are led to recognize the excellence of the Mother of God, and we are moved to a filial love towards our mother and to the imitation of her virtues.[2]

As we discuss devotional prayer to Mary, it is important to recall that we pray to Mary, and relate spiritually to Mary, because we seek her prayers on our behalf. We do not believe that Mary has some power independent of the power of Christ. We do not believe that from Mary we can obtain something Christ cannot give. There is no question of Catholics "worshiping" Mary. On the contrary. To pray to Mary is simply to ask her companionship and support in prayer, for through baptism we are adopted brothers and sisters of Christ, which makes Mary our Mother, and we turn to our Mother to ask for her help in prayer. Much as we would ask our earthly mother to pray for us, so we ask our heavenly Mother to pray for us as well. It's as uncomplicated as that.

May: Mary's Month

Traditionally May is dedicated to Mary as her special month. One of the most important Catholic poets of the modern era, Gerard Manley Hopkins, S.J. (d. 1889), wrote a poem titled "The May Magnificat."

> May is Mary's month, and I
> Muse at that and wonder why....

At length he relates Mary to the springtime rebirth of nature, and then ends:

> This ecstasy all through mothering earth
> Tells Mary her mirth till Christ's birth
> To remember and exultation
> In God who was her salvation.

Special Devotions on a Special Day

Saturday is dedicated to Mary in the Catholic tradition. On virtually any Saturday, a Mass of Our Lady may be said. The idea of setting aside one day of the week for a special focus on Mary makes sense. It simply means that on that day we are reminded to give a little extra attention to the place of Mary in our spirituality and in our relationship with Christ.

The Rosary

Without a doubt, the most popular Catholic devotion of all time is a Marian devotion, the Rosary. As noted in chapter 3, the word *rosary* means rose garden, tied to ancient tradition that Mary is the "rose of Sharon" mentioned in Song of Songs 2:1.

Using a string of beads, or a string with knots tied in it, to count one's prayers has pre-Christian origins. Both Hindus and Buddhists use strings of beads for prayer purposes and were doing so centuries before the birth of Christ.[3] Later, Muslims also used strings of beads as prayer counters. The first Christians to use counters for prayer were most likely the Desert Fathers of the third century. These ascetics, who lived in Syria and

Egypt, sometimes used pebbles to count their prayers.

Some scholars think that twelfth-century Crusaders returning to Europe brought strings of prayer beads from the Holy Land, where they found them used in Islam. This is pure conjecture, however, and there seems to be no tangible evidence to support this theory.

The most popular Catholic tradition about the origin of the Rosary says that in the thirteenth century Mary appeared and gave the rosary beads to St. Dominic, the founder of the Order of Preachers, or Dominicans. But this tradition has no factual basis. The story itself dates from more than two hundred years after the death of Dominic. It is a verifiable fact that St. Dominic had a great devotion to Mary and that he encouraged this same devotion in the men and women who became members of the Dominican order down through the centuries. It is also true that the Dominicans popularized the Rosary devotion and spread it throughout the entire church.

Backtracking a bit, however, the Christian use of rosary beads is older than the Hail Mary prayer, which forms the basis for the modern Rosary devotion. Christians first used strings of beads to count psalms, then to count Our Fathers. Later, the beads were used to count Hail Marys and eventually to count Our Fathers and Hail Marys together in various combinations. Finally, the devotional use developed to the Rosary as we know it today.[4]

The Rosary is a simple form of devotional prayer, but it is not a devotional prayer only for the simple. As David Burton Bryan explains, the Rosary can be used to cultivate a life of deep prayer and contemplation.[5] The Rosary is an appropriate devotional prayer for everyone, regardless of educational level or station in life.

The basic process is easy to explain. The typical Rosary consists of five sets of ten Hail Marys (a short prayer that appears on page 130) interrupted by one recitation of the Our Father (the Lord's Prayer) and one recitation of the Doxology, or "Glory Be" (a short trinitarian prayer). Each "decade," or series of ten Hail Marys, has a "mystery" from the life of Christ or Mary assigned to it. Reading about praying the Rosary may make it seem complicated, but actually praying the Rosary is easy, especially if you start doing so with a group of people who know the prayer. Still, here is a basic description of how to use rosary beads to say the Rosary. Note that the Rosary presumes familiarity with the Gospels.

1. While holding the crucifix recite the Apostles' Creed.
2. Hold the first bead after the crucifix and recite the Our Father.
3. Say one Hail Mary for each of the next three beads—each one, respectively, is for an increase in the theological virtues of faith, hope, and love.
4. On the next bead, recite the Doxology ("Glory Be").
5. Recall the first mystery, depending on which set of mysteries applies to the day. (See the following list of mysteries.) Here is where familiarity with the gospel story is important.
6. For each of the following set of ten beads, recite a Hail Mary. The ideal is to reflect on the mystery for that decade, but the most important thing is for the heart to be turned toward God. If your mind wanders, it's not a big problem; as soon as you realize you are distracted, simply bring your attention back gently to the words of the prayer and to the mystery for that decade. Many love the Rosary because even if the mind wanders, at least the fingers go on praying.
7. After the ten Hail Marys, conclude each decade by saying a

"Glory Be" on the bead between one decade and the next.

8. Using that same bead, begin the next decade by saying the Our Father, then repeat the process through all five decades.

9. At the end of the fifth and final decade, say the final "Glory Be." Then conclude the Rosary by praying the ancient prayer known as the Salve Regina (Hail, Holy Queen):

> Hail, Holy Queen, Mother of Mercy; hail our life, our sweetness, and our hope. To you do we cry, poor banished children of Eve. To you do we send up our sighs, mourning and weeping in this valley of tears. Turn then, most gracious Advocate, your eyes of mercy toward us. And after this our exile, show unto us the blessed fruit of your womb, Jesus. O clement [mercy], O loving, O sweet Virgin Mary.
>
> Pray for us, O holy Mother of God.
>
> That we may become worthy of the promises of Christ.

Some people add the following prayer:

> O God, by the life, death, and resurrection of your only-begotten Son, you purchased for us the rewards of eternal life; grant, we beseech you, that while meditating on these mysteries of the Holy Rosary, we may imitate what they contain and obtain what they promise. Through the same Christ our Lord. Amen.

Sometimes Rosary devotees also add the so-called Miraculous Medal prayer, which originated with the Marian apparitions on the Rue du Bac in 1831:

> O Mary, conceived without sin, pray for us who have recourse to thee.

Following are the mysteries of the Rosary, followed in italics by a scriptural passage to illustrate the origin of each:

The Joyful Mysteries
(Used on Mondays and Thursdays)
  1. The Annunciation
     Then Mary said, "Here am I, the servant of the Lord; let it be with me according to your word" (Luke 1:38).
  2. The Visitation
     In those days Mary set out and went with haste to a Judean town in the hill country, where she entered the house of Zechariah and greeted Elizabeth (Luke 1:39-40).
  3. The Nativity
     And she gave birth to her firstborn son and wrapped him in bands of cloth, and laid him in a manger, because there was no place for them in the inn (Luke 2:7).
  4. The Presentation
     When the time came for their purification according to the law of Moses, they brought him up to Jerusalem to present him to the Lord (Luke 2:22).
  5. The Finding of Jesus in the Temple
     After three days they found him in the temple, sitting among the teachers, listening to them and asking them questions (Luke 2:46).

The Sorrowful Mysteries
(Used on Tuesdays and Fridays)
  1. The Agony in the Garden
     And going a little farther, [Jesus] threw himself on the ground and prayed, "My Father, if it is possible, let this cup pass from me; yet not what I want but what you want" (Matthew 26:39).

2. The Scourging at the Pillar

And after flogging Jesus, [Pilate] handed him over to be crucified (Matthew 27:26b).

3. The Crowning With Thorns

And after twisting some thorns into a crown, they put it on his head. They put a reed in his right hand and knelt before him and mocked him, saying, "Hail, King of the Jews!" (Matthew 27:29).

4. The Carrying of the Cross

So they took Jesus; and carrying the cross by himself, he went out to what is called The Place of the Skull, which in Hebrew is called Golgotha (John 19:16b-17).

5. The Crucifixion and Death of Jesus

And they crucified him (Mark 15:24).

The Glorious Mysteries

(Used on Sundays, Wednesdays, and Saturdays)

1. The Resurrection

He is not here; for he has been raised, as he said (Matthew 28:6).

2. The Ascension

As they were watching, he was lifted up, and a cloud took him out of their sight (Acts 1:9).

3. The Coming of the Holy Spirit

All of them were filled with the Holy Spirit (Acts 2:4).

4. The Assumption of Mary Into Heaven

5. The Coronation of Mary as Queen of Heaven

The fourth and fifth glorious mysteries have no corresponding scriptural references. The traditions behind these two beliefs are ancient in origin, however, and they are a good illustration of the Catholic belief that divine revelation is not limited to Scripture. Rather, Scripture and Sacred Tradition go hand in hand; indeed, it was Sacred Tradition—the ongoing faith experience of the Christian community—that gave birth to the New Testament. Our understanding of divine revelation continues to grow and develop over time.

The Assumption of Mary into heaven and the coronation of

Devotional History of Icons

Where did the earliest artistic representations of Mary come from, and what was their original purpose?

In monastic communities, known for their dedication to the production of icons, making an icon was not thought of as a form of artistic expression. It was, in itself, a form of spiritual devotion. Monks made icons as a way to open themselves to the Spirit of God.

According to legend, the first icons and images of Mary came into existence by supernatural means. They were, it was said, painted by the evangelist Luke, or by the Madonna herself, or at least they were completed by her. To alter this image, the *vera icona*, in the name of artistic freedom would be to deny its divine origin. For the icon as a copy of a divine archetypal image opens up for humans—in and through the veneration of the earthly image—direct access to the space of these images: to the sacred. Thus cultic images lift the person out of his or her earthly world into a higher world.

Caroline H. Ebertshäuser[6]

Mary are beliefs once embraced by all Christians, treasures now preserved by the Roman Catholic tradition. So it is appropriate that they are included in the Rosary along with the specifically scriptural mysteries.

Finally, note that the purpose of the Rosary is not to multiply words in order to wheedle God into something, or in order to get Mary's attention. Rather, the repetitive nature of the Rosary helps to cultivate a spirit of meditative, even contemplative, prayerfulness.

The Angelus and Regina Coeli

The Angelus is a Marian devotion that goes back to about the tenth century in England. Originally, it may have consisted of simply praying three Hail Marys when the church or monastery bell rang for Night Prayer or Compline. The Angelus honors the central mystery of the Christian faith, the Incarnation, God assuming a human nature. The name of this devotion comes from the Latin phrase that begins the prayer: *Angelus Domini*, which means "Angel of the Lord."

Three times a day, particularly in more traditional, rural Catholic societies, and in monastic communities and some religious congregations, church or chapel bells call the faithful to recite this prayer:

> The angel of the Lord declared unto Mary
> And she conceived of the Holy Spirit.
> Hail Mary....

> Behold the handmaid of the Lord.
> Be it done unto me according to thy word.
> Hail Mary....

And the Word was made flesh,
And dwelt among us.
Hail Mary....

Pray for us, Holy Mother of God,
That we may be made worthy of the promises of Christ.

Let us pray. Pour forth, we beg thee, O Lord, thy grace
into our hearts: that we, to whom the Incarnation of
Christ your Son was made known by the message of an
angel, may by his passion and cross be brought to the
glory of his resurrection. Through the same Christ our
Lord. Amen.

During the liturgical season of Easter, the Angelus is replaced
by a similar Marian devotion, the Regina Coeli or Queen of
Heaven:

O Queen of Heaven rejoice, alleluia!
For he whom thou didst merit to bear, alleluia!
Has risen as he said, alleluia!
Pray for us to God, alleluia!

Rejoice and be glad, O Virgin Mary, alleluia!
For the Lord has risen indeed, alleluia!

Let us pray: O God, who gave joy to the world through
the resurrection of thy son, our Lord Jesus Christ: grant
that we may obtain, through his Virgin Mother, Mary, the
joys of everlasting life. Through the same Christ our Lord.
Amen.

Traditional Prayers for the Intercession of Mary

Some of the most cherished prayers in Catholicism are addressed to Mary. In earlier chapters I've discussed a few classical prayers, the Salve Regina or Hail, Holy Queen and the Stabat Mater. Here are a few more of the most popular. Where it seems appropriate, for the sake of the poetry, the version given retains traditional, admittedly archaic words, such as *thee, thy,* and *thou.*[7]

The Hail Mary or Angelic Salutation

The Latin for Hail Mary is Ave Maria. The prayer is often called the Angelic Salutation, as the first line is the address given to Mary by the angel at the Annunciation.

Hail, Mary, full of grace. The Lord is with thee. Blessed art thou among women, and blessed is the fruit of thy womb, Jesus. Holy Mary, Mother of God, pray for us sinners, now and at the hour of our death. Amen.

The Magnificat or Canticle of Mary

See Luke 1:46-55.

My soul magnifies the Lord, and my spirit rejoices in God my Savior, for he has looked with favor on the lowliness of his servant. Surely, from now on all generations will call me blessed; for the Mighty One has done great things for me, and holy is his name. His mercy is for those who fear him from generation to generation. He has shown strength with his arm; he has scattered the proud in the thoughts of their hearts. He has brought down the powerful from their thrones, and lifted up the lowly; he has filled the hungry with good things, and sent the rich away empty. He has helped his servant Israel, in remembrance of his mercy, according to the promise he made to our ancestors, to Abraham and to his descendants forever.

The Memorare

This prayer was written by St. Bernard of Clairvaux (d. 1153), founder of the Cistercian order and a mystical theologian of great prominence.

Remember, O most gracious Virgin Mary, that never was it known that anyone who fled to thy protection, implored thy help, or sought thy intercession was left unaided. Inspired by this confidence I fly into thee, O Virgin of virgins, my mother. To thee do I come, before thee I stand, sinful and sorrowful. O Mother of the Word Incarnate, despise not my petitions, but in thy mercy hear and answer me. Amen.

Alma Redemptoris Mater (*Loving Mother of the Redeemer*)

O loving Mother of the Redeemer, Gate of Heaven, Star of the Sea, assist your people who have fallen, yet strive to rise again. To the wonder of nature, you bore your Creator, yet remained a Virgin, after as before, you who received Gabriel's joyful greeting, have pity on us poor sinners. Amen.

Prayer to Our Lady of Guadalupe

Our Lady of Guadalupe, mystical Rose, intercede for Holy Church, protect the Holy Father, help all who turn to you in their needs, and, since you are the ever Virgin Mary and Mother of the true God, obtain for us from your most holy Son, the grace of keeping our faith, sweet hope in the midst of the trials of life, burning charity, and the precious gift of final perseverance. Amen.

The Litany of the Blessed Virgin

A litany is a—usually rather long—list of invocational prayers. A litany is *not* based on a belief that by the sheer multiplication of words one has a better chance of getting God's attention. Rather, the purpose of a litany is to establish a rhythmic atmosphere of prayer in order to cultivate the spirit of prayer on a deeper level. In this sense, a litany is similar to the Rosary.

The Litany of the Blessed Virgin originated about eight hundred years ago and was approved in 1587 by Pope Sixtus V. Since then other popes have made several additions. Although a litany may be prayed by yourself, generally the ideal is for a leader to read the invocation with a group responding. Here is an abbreviated version of the Litany of the Blessed Virgin:[8]

Lord, have mercy.
Lord, have mercy.
Christ, have mercy.
Christ, have mercy.
Lord, have mercy.
Lord, have mercy.
God our Father in heaven,
have mercy on us (repeat after each of the following invocations)
God the Son, Redeemer of the world ...
God the Holy Spirit ...
Holy Trinity, one God ...
Holy Mary,
pray for us (repeat after each of the following invocations)
Holy Mother of God ...
Most Honored of Virgins ...
Mother of Christ ...

Mother of the Church ...
Mother of Divine Grace ...
Mother Most Pure ...
Mother of Chaste Love ...
Mother and Virgin ...
Sinless Mother ...
Dearest of Mothers ...
Model of Motherhood ...
Mother of Good Counsel ..
Mother of Our Creator ...
Mother of Our Savior ...
Mirror of Justice ...
Seat of Wisdom ...
Cause of Our Joy ...
Spiritual Vessel ...
Vessel of Honor ...
Shrine of the Spirit ...
Vessel of Selfless Devotion ...
Mystical Rose ...
Tower of David ...
Tower of Ivory ...
House of Gold ...
Ark of the Covenant ...
Gate of Heaven ...
Morning Star ...
Health of the Sick ...
Queen of Angels ...
Queen of Patriarchs and Prophets ...
Queen of Apostles and Martyrs ...
Queen of Peace ...
Lamb of God, you take away the sins of the world,

have mercy on us (repeat after each of the following invocations)

Lamb of God, you take away the sins of the world ...

Lamb of God, you take away the sins of the world ...

Pray for us, holy Mother of God,

That we may become worthy of the promises of Christ.

Let us pray. Grant, we beg thee, Lord, that we your people enjoy constant health in mind and body. Through the intercession of the Virgin Mary free us from the sorrows of this life and lead us to happiness in the life to come. Grant this through Christ our Lord. Amen.

There are other ancient and more modern litanies to Mary, such as an eighteenth-century litany of the Immaculate Heart of Mary and a newly approved (1981) Litany in Honor of the Queenship of Mary.

Devotional Discoveries

Much of this chapter has focused on traditional, formal prayer and reflection about Mary. But throughout this whole book, I've sprinkled here and there comments by saints, hymn writers, and devotional writers that can serve to draw one's heart to the lessons we learn from Mary. American novelist Mary Gordon says: "I think ... it is through poetry, through painting, sculpture, music ... by virtue of the labor, craft, and genius of their great creators, that one finds the surest way back to the Mother of God."[9]

Two devotional anthologies on Mary are *Mornings With Mary* and *Marian Prayer Book.*[10]

A Normative Document for Marian Devotions

It is important to note that in his 1974 apostolic exhortation, *Marialis Cultus,* Pope Paul VI laid the groundwork for modern devotion to Mary. He said that honoring Mary should happen within the limitations of a healthy, balanced Christian faith. Such a devotion should never become more important than faith in the one triune God: Father, Son, and Holy Spirit. It should always be conscious that only Christ is the Savior, and he alone is the one Mediator between God and humankind. Devotion to Mary should give proper recognition to the action

What Is the Scriptural Rosary?

One variation on the traditional Rosary incorporates brief readings from Scripture into the Rosary devotion itself. Typically, this means reading or reciting words from Scripture that are relevant to the mystery for each decade prior to praying each Hail Mary. Some versions of the Scriptural Rosary also add new sets of mysteries to the traditional joyful, sorrowful, and glorious mysteries. For example, in *The Seven-Day Scriptural Rosary,* Larry London provides "Healing Mysteries" to be prayed on Wednesdays, "Eucharistic Mysteries" to be prayed on Thursdays, and "Consoling Mysteries" to be prayed on Saturdays.[11]

Many people appreciate this form of the Rosary. Its only drawback is that a little book is needed to follow all the scriptural texts, so either you must hold the book in one hand and the beads in the other, which can be a bit unwieldy, or set aside the rosary beads and pray without them.

of the Holy Spirit in the gift of divine grace. Finally, devotion to Mary should always reflect the renewed awareness of the relationship between Mary and the church, that is, that Mary is a model of the church and of all that the church is called to be.

Devotion to Mary should also be permeated with the Scriptures and the great scriptural themes, and because the liturgy is the ultimate norm of all Christian spirituality and piety, devotion to Mary should be in tune with the liturgy's spirit, themes, and seasons. These guidelines should be used to evaluate the value of both traditional Marian devotional practices and the formation of new ones.

CHAPTER EIGHT

Mary the Model Disciple for a New Millennium

Christians down through the centuries have understood Mary in many and varied ways. As Christians move into a new millennium, it makes sense that we would ask ourselves how Mary can help guide us in our continuing pilgrimage of faith, how Mary can help Christians be better disciples of Christ, her son and God's Son. Perhaps we would do well to return to some basic images of Mary and interpret them for a new era: Mary the young woman of faith; Mary the pilgrim; Mary the questioner; Mary at the foot of the cross; Mary the prayerful disciple; Mary in the Immaculate Conception; and Mary in her assumption.

Mary, Young Woman of Faith

The Gospel of Luke gives us a young woman, a girl by our standards, who responds to God in wholehearted faith. She has her questions, and she asks her questions, but the answers she receives do not make things crystal clear. Nevertheless, Mary takes the word of an angel on faith; she agrees to be the instrument of God's saving love in the world without knowing what that actually means. She entrusts herself to God's will, trusting that being in God's will is all that she will ever need or want.

Mary teaches us that faith is, above all, a personal relationship with God in Christ, a personal relationship that does not demand to know what the future will bring. Instead, this faith abandons the self in complete trust that, whatever happens,

God's loving kindness will "be there." It is this faith that Mary teaches us yesterday, today, and forever. This is not an easy faith but a faith that, like the gospel, both comforts and challenges.

The faith and trust Mary models for us is not merely theoretical. It is the kind of faith and trust in God required, for example, of anyone who would commit him- or herself to God by making a commitment to another imperfect human being in marriage. It is the kind of faith and trust in God required of a man who becomes a priest or of anyone who would embrace the vowed religious life in a monastic order or a religious congregation.

As a model of faith, Mary comforts us with a mother's love. She reassures us by her example and by her presence that the faith she models is a worthy and attainable ideal. For in Christ, her son, we can be alive with a faith that is bigger than ourselves, a faith of which, on our own, we are incapable. In Christ, Mary reminds us, we can live a faith that makes us both "free from …" and "free to …."

The gift of faith that comes from the risen Lord frees us *from* fear, anxiety, and worry. We need no longer fear that the worst will happen, because it never will. Even "the worst" that this world knows—death itself—is an invitation to abandon ourselves in complete trust to God's love. Faith frees us from constant anxiety as a way of life. Even after the wondrous events of the Annunciation, Mary had plenty she could have worried about. Instead, she acted in trust even when she was clueless.

Faith also frees us *to* act on behalf of faith, in hope, for the sake of love. The faith Mary models for us is a faith empowered to step out, stand up, and serve others. Mary could have stayed at home with her wonderful secret. Instead, she rushed to be at Elizabeth's side, to share and to care. She noticed at the wedding at Cana that the wine casks were empty. Mary's focus was not on herself but on the needs of others, and faith liberates us to do the same.

Mary the Pilgrim

Joseph is the central actor in the Gospel of Matthew's infancy narrative. Yet, although silent, Mary is center stage as well. When Joseph rouses her in the night to flee to Egypt, she could balk. Instead, she accepts the life of a pilgrim, really a refugee. She has never been to Egypt before, a foreign land. With complete trust in God's loving care, she heads into the unknown for the sake of her newborn son. She believed that, whatever the future might bring, it could only be a journey into God's love.

As we trek into the unknown of a new century, we have no idea what the future may bring. Young Mary beckons us to abandon fear and anxiety and step out with confidence. For ultimately the future is God's unconditional love. With a smile on her lips, she whispers words of encouragement: Fear not, step out. Whatever the future may bring, be assured that it will be a journey into God's love, in ways you can't even begin to imagine. So step out.

The life of a pilgrim, a refugee in time, if you will, is, again, a life of "freedom from" and "freedom to." It has its inconveniences, true. It has its uncertainties. Sacrifices are required. But if, with Mary, we expect God's love to be present in each day, active in whatever happens and whatever we face, then inconveniences, uncertainties, and sacrifices become little more than empty spaces where God's love can move in and take over. Empty spaces where God's love can move in and take over in ways we can't begin to imagine.

Mary the Questioner

Mary shows us, in more ways than one, that faith doesn't mean never asking questions or never having doubts. From moment one, when the angel gives Mary an earful, she has her questions. How can this be? She has her questions, and she asks them.

Centuries later, in a cosmic shift that, all the same, has its clear continuities, Mary as Our Lady of Guadalupe, and Mary as Our Lady of Lourdes, and so forth, always, always, receives the questions of startled, amazed visionaries with complete equanimity. According to every report, Mary has no problem with questions, even though her answers don't seem to clear up everything right away for all concerned.

Mary shows us that faith and questions are compatible. Faith and doubt are compatible, too. After all, faith relates us, finite beings, to God, who is infinite. When you bring together the finite and the infinite, the finite side of the relationship is bound to have some questions, being unable to completely grasp the infinite. So ask away, and doubt away, and tell the Lord Jesus all about it, and tell Mary all about it, and remain open, listening.

Like Mary, however, do not be surprised if the answers you get do not add up to scientifically precise explanations. When the Infinite answers the questions of the finite, those answers are still likely to leave you scratching your head. Those answers still require faith and trust, just as the answers Mary received still required faith and trust from her. The very same way.

Mary at the Foot of the Cross

John 19:26-27 gives us that dramatic and touching scene where Jesus speaks to his mother and "the beloved disciple" from the cross of his execution.

Mary for the New Millennium

How might devotion to Mary fit into Catholic spirituality for the new millennium?

Mary at the beginning of the third millennium still accompanies the church on her pilgrimage of faith and is having a profound influence on the church. Her "Magnificat spirituality" is becoming more and more the spirituality of the church. The great renewal movements in the church have come under the direction and inspiration of her presence....

Mary, risen and glorified in body and soul, is present in the church and with us as our Mother. We can get to know and love her better; we can open the home of our hearts and make a place for Mary our mother; we can allow her song, her spirituality, to become our own song and our own spirituality; we can, above all, imitate God the Father and entrust ourselves completely to Mary. Then our devotion to Mary will be truly based on God's word and we will begin to live deeply and joyfully by the last word, the very last word that Jesus spoke to the disciple on earth: She is your mother.

Jim McManus, C.S.S.R. [1]

When Jesus saw his mother and the disciple whom he loved standing beside her, he said to his mother, "Woman, here is your son."

Then he said to the disciple, "Here is your mother." And from that hour the disciple took her into his own home.

Mary at the foot of the cross stands helplessly as her son dies a horrible death. Any mother or father who has had to witness the suffering of a son or daughter can identify with Mary in this situation. She stands as a model in more ways than one. Think of what many a parent might have said in such a situation. "You brought this on yourself. Why did you do it—to yourself? To me?" But not Mary. She stands in silence.

Perhaps she is long past trying to understand. All she can do is stand and watch. Chances are, she is as clueless as anyone else. In the darkness of her own soul, she must trust that somehow it will all make sense in the end. She has faith and trust in the face of overwhelming absurdity, faith and trust in the face of complete disaster. Mary is a model of faith for anyone who sees nothing but dark meaninglessness.

Mary the Prayerful Disciple

Mary appears once in the Acts of the Apostles, after Jesus' ascension, and she speaks only by her actions. "All these were constantly devoting themselves to prayer, together with certain women, including Mary the mother of Jesus" (1:14).

The Mary of this brief scene is (a) with the other disciples of Jesus, not off someplace by herself, and (b) with the others, giving herself to "constant" prayer. Mary is among the disciples, herself a disciple. She belongs, and she is welcome. At the same time, we must acknowledge that the other disciples do not turn to her in her son's absence. They do not try to make her fill Jesus' sandals, as it were; they do not urge her to speak for him. They do not make her their new leader. They do not even appoint her a special adviser to Peter, who clearly has a unique position of leadership as the account unfolds in Acts. Neither does the Mary of the Acts of the Apostles get pushy in any way.

She does not try to assert herself as her son's representative; she does not try to speak for him. She simply joins the other disciples in prayer. She simply belongs, neither greater nor lesser than any of the other disciples.

The Mary we find here is a model of faith that expresses itself in prayer *with others*. Mary is not isolating herself in a cave. Neither has she given herself over to despair. She is with the others, and by her quiet, prayerful presence she becomes a model of what prayer means for the disciples of Jesus. Prayer, even in private, is always *with others*. Even when we pray alone, we pray with the communion of saints in this world and in eternity. Mary prays, not knowing what to expect. Once again, she is primarily the model of faith and trust, this time a faith expressed in constant prayer.

Mary could have involved herself in any number of busy occupations at a time like this. Instead, she joins the other disciples in constant prayer. Mary shows that prayer is fundamental to discipleship. Prayer has meaning in any circumstances.

Mary in Her Immaculate Conception

What possible meaning can the Immaculate Conception, Mary's being conceived in her mother's womb free from the effects of original sin, have for today? One theologian comments, on the dogma of the Immaculate Conception, that it "shows that God can be, and is, utterly gracious toward us, not by reason of our merits but by reason of divine love and mercy alone."[2]

In other words, the Immaculate Conception is living human proof of how total and unconditional is God's love. By causing Mary to be conceived in her mother's womb free from original sin, so that his own Son might be born of a sinless mother, God shows how deep is his love for us.

Yet another theologian explains: "The dogma of Mary's original sinlessness.... signifies the good news that for the church and for every human being, grace is more original than sin."[2]

Devotion to Mary in her Immaculate Conception is devotion to God's freely given victory over evil in Christ. The dogma of the Immaculate Conception is a sign of this victory,[3] as if God speaks, saying, *See what I can and will do for you, my people?*

In the long run, when the final tally is counted, sin will count for nothing; grace will be all. That is the meaning of the Immaculate Conception. From this perspective, the nineteenth-century English poet William Wordsworth's description of Mary is right on the money. He called Mary "our tainted nature's solitary boast."

Mary in Her Assumption

The dogma of the Assumption reaffirms what we already know from the resurrection of Christ, that salvation is not just a spiritual matter but one that involves our bodies, as well, in a new state that perfectly unites body and soul. In her assumption, Mary teaches us that the life of faith is not a mere discipline that requires us to scorn and ignore the body to cultivate the soul. Rather, the body is an equal player, as it were, in the life of discipleship. What concerns the soul concerns the body, and what concerns the body concerns the soul.

Where would we be, and what would we accomplish in the world, if we did not have bodies, if we were not bodies? At the same time, what would we do without the essence of our being that we call the soul? Both are required, and both will share, somehow, in our ultimate eternal destiny. That is the message of the Assumption. Devotion to Mary in her assumption is devotion to Christ in his resurrection and a reaffirmation of our union with him through baptism.

Finally, it only remains to say that devotion to Mary, for all its varied forms according to culture, history, and place, is a characteristic of Catholic life that goes back to the beginnings of the Christian community and the origins of the church. Let us take St. Bernard of Clairvaux's words in the twelfth century, then, as our inspiration for the twenty-first century:

> Let us not imagine that we obscure the glory of the Son by the praise we lavish on the Mother; for the more she is honored, the greater is the glory of her Son.[5]

NOTES

Introduction

1. Jaroslav Pelikan, *Mary Through the Centuries: Her Place in the History of Culture* (New York: Yale University Press, 1996), 1–2.
2. Mary A. Donovan, "Communion of Saints," in *The HarperCollins Encyclopedia of Catholicism,* ed. Richard P. McBrien (San Francisco: HarperSanFrancisco, 1995), 339.
3. The term comes from the 1943 encyclical of Pius XII, *Mystici Corporis.*
4. Donovan, 339.
5. *Catechism of the Catholic Church,* n. 2674-2675.
6. John W. Miller, *Calling God "Father": Essays on the Bible, Fatherhood, and Culture* (Mahwah, N.J.: Paulist Press, 1999), 5. Italics are in original text.
7. Quoted in Rhonda DeSola Chervin, *Quotable Saints* (Ann Arbor, Mich.: Servant Publications, 1992), 100.

Chapter 1

1. Dates for writing of biblical books are from Raymond E. Brown, S.S., et al., ed., *The New Jerome Biblical Commentary* (Englewood Cliffs, N.J.: Prentice Hall, 1990).
2. Benedict T. Viviano, O.P., "The Gospel According to Matthew," in *The New Jerome Biblical Commentary,* 636.
3. Brown, *The New Jerome Biblical Commentary;* see also Raymond E. Brown, S.S., *An Introduction to the New Testament* (New York: Doubleday, 1997), 274: "the best date would seem to be *85, give or take five to ten years.*"
4. *The Catholic Study Bible—The New American Bible* (New York: Oxford University Press, 1990), Luke 2:7 n.
5. Robert J. Karris, O.F.M., "The Gospel According to Luke," in *The New Jerome Biblical Commentary,* 684.
6. *Catechism of the Catholic Church,* n. 500.
7. Pheme Perkins, "The Gospel According to John," in *The New Jerome Biblical Commentary,* 954.
8. Perkins, 954.
9. Perkins, 982.
10. Raymond E. Brown, S.S., *Responses to 101 Questions on the Bible*

(Mahwah, N.J.: Paulist Press, 1990), 93.

11. Sally Cunneen, *In Search of Mary: The Woman and the Symbol* (New York: Ballantine, 1996), 57.

12. Adela Yarbo Collins, "The Apocalypse (Revelation)," in *The New Jerome Biblical Commentary*, 1008.

13. For an extensive discussion of Old Testament texts later interpreted as prophetic references to Mary, see Jaroslav Pelikan, *Mary Through the Centuries: Her Place in the History of Culture* (New York: Yale University Press, 1996), chap. 2.

14. *The Catholic Study Bible*, Genesis 3:15 n.

15. Joseph Jensen, O.S.B., "Isaiah 1-39," in *The New Jerome Biblical Commentary*, 235.

Chapter 2

1. Luigi Gambero, *Mary and the Fathers of the Church: The Blessed Virgin Mary in Patristic Thought*, trans. Thomas Buffer (San Francisco: Ignatius Press, 1999), 28.

2. "Letters of Ignatius: Ephesians," 19:1, in *Early Christian Fathers*, ed. Cyril C. Richardson (New York: Macmillan, 1970). The following quotations from Ignatius' letters are all from this source.

3. For information on the two earliest images of Mary, I rely on Sally Cunneen, *In Search of Mary: The Woman and the Symbol* (New York: Ballantine, 1996), 63–75.

4. Wilhelm Schneemelcher, ed., *New Testament Apocrypha*, trans. Robert McLachlan Wilson, rev. ed., 2 vols. (Louisville, Ky.: Westminster/John Knox Press, 1991–93), 1:429.

5. Cunneen, 66.

6. Quoted in Cunneen, 66.

7. Quoted in Cunneen, 68.

8. James Hamilton Charlesworth, trans., "Ode 19," *The Odes of Solomon: The Syriac Texts* (Missoula, Mont.: Scholars Press, 1978), 82–83, quoted in Cunneen, 62.

9. Cunneen, 62.

10. John R. Shinners, "The Cult of Mary and Popular Belief," in *Mary, Woman of Nazareth*, ed. Doris Donnelly (Mahwah, N.J.: Paulist Press, 1989), 163.

11. Ronald F. Hock, trans., *The Life of Mary and Birth of Jesus: The Ancient Infancy Gospel of James* (Berkeley, Calif.: Ulysses Press, 1997). The following summary is based on and quotations are from this

source.

12. This summary is based on a modern, beautifully illustrated retelling of this legend geared to children: Tomie dePaola, *The Clown of God* (New York: Harcourt Brace, 1978).

13. Jaroslav Pelikan, *Mary Through the Centuries: Her Place in the History of Culture* (New York: Yale University Press, 1996), 47.

14. Pelikan, 47.

15. Summaries of the Brothers Grimm stories of Mary adapted from Joe H. Kirchberger, "Mary in Literature," in *Mary: Art, Culture, and Religion Through the Ages,* ed. Caroline H. Ebertshäuser et al. (New York: Crossroad, 1998), 106–7.

16. Cunneen, 69.

Chapter 3

1. Quoted in Joe H. Kirchberger, "Mary in Literature," in *Mary: Art, Culture and Religion Through the Ages,* ed. Caroline H. Ebertshäuser, et al. (New York: Crossroad, 1998), 60.

2. Everett Ferguson, "Origen," in *Eerdman's Handbook to the History of Christianity* (Grand Rapids, Mich.: Eerdmans, 1977), 104.

3. Quoted in Kirchberger, 60.

4. Quoted in John Rotelle, O.S.A., ed., *Mary's Yes: Meditations on Mary Through the Ages* (Ann Arbor, Mich.: Servant Publications, 1988), 29.

5. Quoted in Leo Donald Davis, S.J., *The First Seven Ecumenical Councils (325–787): Their History and Theology* (Wilmington, Del.: Michael Glazier, 1987), 161–62.

6. Gerald O'Collins, S.J., and Edward G. Farrugia, S.J., *A Concise Dictionary of Theology* (Mahwah, N.J.: Paulist Press, 1991), 138.

7. Quoted in Mary E. Hines, "Mary," in *The New Dictionary of Catholic Spirituality,* ed. Michael Downey (Collegeville, Minn.: Liturgical Press, 1993), 636.

8. Quoted in Hines, 637.

9. Quoted in Rotelle, 47.

10. Elizabeth A. Johnson, "Blessed Virgin Mary," in *The HarperCollins Encyclopedia of Catholicism,* ed. Richard P. McBrien (San Francisco: HarperSanFrancisco, 1995), 834.

11. Kirchberger, 72.

12. Quoted in Luigi Gambero, *Mary and the Fathers of the Church,* trans. Thomas Buffer (San Francisco: Ignatius Press, 1999), 353.

13. Quoted in Rotelle, 42–43.

14. Quoted in Evelyn Bence, comp. *Quiet Moments With Hildegard and the Women Mystics* (Ann Arbor, Mich.: Servant Publications, 1999), 10.
15. Marina Warner, *Alone of All Her Sex* (London: Quartet Books, 1978), 86–87.
16. Quoted in Gambero, 397.
17. Benedict Groeschel, C.F.R., *Stumbling Blocks, Stepping Stones* (Mahwah, N.J.: Paulist Press, 1987), 145.
18. Kirchberger, 80.
19. Quoted in Rotelle, 65.
20. Quoted in Kirchberger, 85.
21. Therese Johnson Borchard, *Our Catholic Devotions: A Popular Guidebook* (New York: Crossroad, 1998), 20.
22. Fr. Richard Beyer, *Blessed Art Thou* (Notre Dame, Ind.: Ave Maria Press, 1996), 224.
23. Warner, 200.
24. Quoted in Charles Dickson, *A Protestant Pastor Looks at Mary* (Huntington, Ind.: Our Sunday Visitor, 1996), 20.
25. Quoted in Hines, 638.
26. Bence, intro. to Mary of Agreda, np.

Chapter 4

1. Benedict Groeschel, C.F.R., *A Still, Small Voice: A Practical Guide on Reported Revelations* (San Francisco: Ignatius Press, 1993), 160.
2. Matthew Bunson, ed., *2000 Our Sunday Visitor's Catholic Almanac* (Huntington, Ind.: Our Sunday Visitor, 1999), 144–45, cites the seven as: Banneux, Belgium (1933), Beauraing, Belgium (1932–33), Fátima, Portugal (1917), Guadalupe, Mexico (1531), La Salette, France (1846), Lourdes, France (1858), and the Rue de Bac, Paris, France (1830).
3. Pamela Moran, *Marian Prayer Book* (Ann Arbor, Mich.: Servant Publications, 1991), 183.
4. The primary source for the material in this section is Stafford Poole, C.M., *Our Lady of Guadalupe: The Origins and Sources of a Mexican National Symbol, 1531–1797* (Tucson, Ariz.: University of Arizona Press, 1996).
5. Quoted in Beyer, 349.
6. Beyer, 352.
7. *Liturgy of the Hours.* See Morning Prayer in the "Common of the Blessed Virgin Mary."

8. *Liturgy of the Hours.* See Morning Prayer in the "Common of the Blessed Virgin Mary."
9. McBrien, 1107.
10. Beyer, 396–97.
11. Richard P. McBrien, *Catholicism,* rev. ed. (San Francisco: HarperSanFrancisco, 1994), 269.

Chapter 5

1. Sally Cunneen, *In Search of Mary: The Woman and the Symbol* (New York: Ballantine Books, 1996), 227.
2. Quoted in Cunneen, 228.
3. Quoted in Cunneen, 230.
4. John R. Donahue, "Dogma," in *The HarperCollins Encyclopedia of Catholicism,* ed. Richard P. McBrien (San Francisco: HarperSanFrancisco, 1995), 425.
5. Elizabeth Johnson, "Immaculate Conception," in *The HarperCollins Encyclopedia of Catholicism,* ed. Richard P. McBrien (San Francisco: HarperSanFrancisco, 1995), 655.
6. Quoted in Hilda Graef, *Mary* (Westminster, Md.: Christian Classics, 1985), 2:113.
7. *"Lumen Gentium,* Dogmatic Constitution on the Church," in *Vatican Council II: The Conciliar and Post Conciliar Documents,* new rev. ed., ed. Austin Flannery, O.P. (Northport, N.Y.: 1992), n. 62.
8. Elizabeth Johnson, "Assumption of the Blessed Virgin Mary," in *The HarperCollins Encyclopedia of Catholicism,* 105.
9. The following quotes are from *Lumen Gentium,* n. 53–63.
10. Thomas Merton, *New Seeds of Contemplation* (New York: New Directions, 1961), 171-72.
11. Karl Rahner, *The Content of Faith: The Best of Karl Rahner's Theological Writings,* ed. Karl Lehmann and Albert Raffelt; trans. ed. Harvey D. Eagan, S.J. (New York: Crossroad, 1992), 452.
12. *Lumen Gentium,* n. 62.
13. Mary E. Hines, "Mary," in *The New Dictionary of Catholic Spirituality,* ed. Michael Downey (Collegeville, Minn.: Liturgical Press, 1993), 641.
14. *Marialis Cultus,* intro.
15. Third General Conference of the Latin American Episcopate, *Evangelization in Latin America's Present and Future* (Puebla, 1979). Quoted in Hines, 643.

16. Leonardo Boff, *The Maternal Face of God* (New York: Harper & Row, 1987), 297.

17. Hines, 644.

18. Raymond E. Brown, S.S., et al., *Mary in the New Testament* (Mahwah, N.J.: Paulist Press, 1978).

19. These titles were originated by Pax Christi, USA. See Hines, 644.

20. Andrew M. Greeley, *The Mary Myth* (New York: Seabury Press, 1977).

21. Four other books make noteworthy contributions to a renewed Mariology and are worth consulting: Frederick M. Jelly, O.P., *Madonna: Mary in the Catholic Tradition* (Huntington, Ind.: Our Sunday Visitor, 1986); Kathleen Coyle, *Mary in the Christian Tradition: From a Contemporary Perspective* (Mystic, Conn.: Twenty-Third Publications, 1996); Alfred McBride, O.Praem, *Images of Mary* (Cincinnati: St. Anthony Messenger, 1999); Jim McManus, C.Ss.R., *All Generations Will Call Me Blessed: Mary at the Millennium* (New York: Crossroad, 1999).

22. Elizabeth A. Johnson, "Blessed Virgin Mary," in *The HarperCollins Encyclopedia of Catholicism*, 838.

Chapter 6

1. *Catechism of the Catholic Church*, n. 971.

2. Marina Warner, *Alone of All Her Sex* (London: Quartet Books, 1976), 240–41.

3. "The Virgin of the Immaculate Conception," quoted in *Her Face: Images of the Virgin Mary in Art*, ed. Marion Wheeler (Cobb, Calif.: First Glance Books, 1998), 21.

4. The Second Vatican Council recovered this ancient insight. See *Lumen Gentium* (Dogmatic Constitution on the Church), n. 11; *Gaudium et Spes* (Pastoral Constitution on the Church in the Modern World), n. 48; and *Apostoicam Actuositatem* (Decree on the Apostolate of Lay People), n. 11.

5. Pope John Paul II, *The Pope Speaks to the American Church* (San Francisco: HarperSanFrancisco, 1992), 223.

6. Warner, 66.

7. Quoted in Michael Buckley, *Catholic Morning Prayers* (Ann Arbor, Mich.: Servant Publications, 2000), 152.

8. Quoted in Paul Thigpen, comp., *The Prayers of Pope John Paul II* (Ann

Arbor, Mich.: Servant Publications, 1996), 223–24.

9. See Rev. Peter Klein, *The Catholic Source Book*, 3d ed. (Dubuque, Iowa: Brown Roa, 1999), 242–43.

10. Quoted in Richard Beyer, *Blessed Art Thou* (Notre Dame, Ind.: Ave Maria Press, 1996), 275.

11. Warner, 218–19.

12. Quoted in Warner, 218.

Chapter 7

1. Therese Johnson Borchard, *Our Catholic Devotions: A Popular Guidebook* (New York: Crossroad, 1998), 13.

2. *"Lumen Gentium,* Dogmatic Constitution on the Church," in *Vatican Council II: The Conciliar and Post Conciliar Documents,* new rev. ed., ed. Austin Flannery, O.P. (Northport, N.Y.: 1992), n. 67.

3. Richard Gribble, C.S.C., *The History and Devotion of the Rosary* (Huntington, Ind.: Our Sunday Visitor, 1992), 10.

4. For a detailed discussion of the development of the Rosary, see Gribble.

5. David Burton Bryan, *A Western Way of Meditation: The Rosary Revisited* (Chicago: Loyola Press, 1991).

6. Caroline H. Ebertshäuser, "Mary in Art," in *Mary: Art, Culture, and Religion Through the Ages,* ed. Caroline H. Ebertshäuser et al. (New York: Crossroad, 1997), 216.

7. See Mitch Finley, "Of Thee (and Thy, and Thou) I Sing." *America,* February 4, 1989, 76.

8. The complete Litany of the Blessed Virgin may be found in various Catholic devotional books, including Msgr. Charles J. Dollen, ed., *Traditional Catholic Prayers* (Huntington, Ind.: Our Sunday Visitor, 1990).

9. Mary Gordon, "Coming to Terms With Mary," *Commonweal,* January 15, 1982, 14.

10. Evelyn Bence, *Mornings With Mary* (Ann Arbor, Mich.: Servant Publications, 1997); Pamela Moran, *Marian Prayer Book* (Ann Arbor, Mich.: Servant Publications, 1991).

11. Larry London, *The Seven-Day Scriptural Rosary* (Huntington, Ind.: Our Sunday Visitor, 1989).

Chapter 8

1. Jim McManus, C.Ss.R., *All Generations Will Call Me Blessed: Mary at the Millennium* (New York: Crossroad, 1999), 175–76.
2. Richard P. McBrien, *Catholicism,* new ed. (San Francisco: HarperSanFrancisco, 1994), 1101.
3. Elizabeth Johnson, "Immaculate Conception," in *The HarperCollins Encyclopedia of Catholicism,* ed. Richard P. McBrien (San Francisco: HarperSanFrancisco, 1995), 656.
4. Johnson, 656.
5. Quoted in Tony Castle, ed., *The New Book of Christian Quotations* (New York: Crossroad, 1989), 158.